CIRCLE
OF
IRON

A Novel by
ROBERT WEVERKA

Based on a Screenplay by
STIRLING SILLIPHANT and STANLEY MANN

Based on an idea by
STIRLING SILLIPHANT and JAMES COBURN
and BRUCE LEE

WARNER BOOKS

A Warner Communications Company

WARNER BOOKS EDITION

ISBN 0-446-89928-3

Warner Books, Inc., 75 Rockefeller Plaza, New York, N.Y. 10019

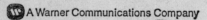 A Warner Communications Company

Printed in the United States of America

Not associated with Warner Press, Inc. of Anderson, Indiana

First Printing: February, 1979

10 9 8 7 6 5 4 3 2 1

"I won!"

cried Cord. "You have given the Medallion to the wrong man."

"I made no error," the wise man in the white robe replied. "You resorted to Hard Contact. There are rules to the combat, and you broke them. Who are you and where do you come from that you could be so uninformed? To what group do you belong?"

"I am Cord," the fighter answered, holding his temper with difficulty. "I belong to no group. I am my own man."

From the assembled spectators an angry murmur arose, and Cord moderated his belligerent tone. "I've come a long way to compete for the right to find Zetan and defeat him—and to see the Book he guards."

"What do you know of this book?"

"Only that it's a book that contains the wisdom of the world."

"The man who is chosen to find and defeat Zetan," said the elder, "must be able to bind an elephant with a spider's web, not stun it with a kick. Your opponent has control. You are not yet the tempered weapon we need. He is the one we shall send."

"One question," Cord demanded. "Why have all the others you've sent never returned?"

"No one knows. Zetan has so far been invincible."

"I will beat this invincible man," Cord vowed, "and I will see what is in the book!"

CIRCLE
OF
IRON

I

The eastern horizon was a blazing streak of red that slowly broadened into orange and yellow. Above, the leaden sky dissolved into paler shades of gray and finally became transparent as the first blinding rays of the sun pierced the creviced ridges of the mountain range.

The endless expanse of valleys and gorges and tumbling mountains seemed barren as the shadows receded and the first touch of morning heat began to burn off the layers of mist.

The old man stood high on a mountainside, barely discernible in the mottling of gray-grown rocks. His head was tilted and at his lips he held a long bamboo flute. The sounds of the flute were soft, yet they were rich and textured and seemed to come from the depths of the earth as the eerie notes danced and drifted into the lower canyons.

It was a plaintive song, calling to the sun and the stars and the farthest reaches of the infinite.

The old man did not seem to move. But a moment later his hand was resting gently on his staff and the sounds of the flute were no more than an echo. He appeared to be listening. Then his face rose quietly to the heavens.

The first caravan to arrive came from the north. The fourteen men rode shaggy ponies, and their heavy jackets and peaked hats were lined with fur. They set up camp at the bottom of the mountain, directly under the monastery.

Two more groups arrived within the hour. The first came on foot; ten yellow-skinned men in gold-embroidered robes. At the rear of the group, six men in loincloths pulled wooden carts loaded with camp equipment. Immediately behind them was a group of black men on horses. They were huge, muscular men with shaven heads and brass bands on their arms. The two groups split as they approached the base of the mountain, one settling far to the left and the other far to the right.

Through the remainder of the afternoon, the road was glutted with new arrivals. Most came on foot, but there were mules and oxen and camels, and some rode huge Arabian steeds with feathered plumes and ornate saddles. There were black men and white men, Turks, Orientals, Mongols, Magyars, Indians, and mixed groups impossible to classify.

By sunset the area was a solid mass of tents and huts and improvised lean-tos, and the din of voices and clatter of cooking utensils mixed with the braying and snorting of animals. Lifelong ene-

mies avoided each other, and the various grou[p]
eyed their neighbors with circumspection. For the
next twenty-four hours they would live in a sus-
pended state of harmony, and they would abide
by the centuries-old traditions of the monastery.

At dusk, a single traveler appeared on the
road. He was a young man—a tall, muscular Caucasian carrying only a hide pouch over his shoulder. His brown hair was bleached from the sun,
and his arms and legs were bronzed and dusty
from his many days of traveling.

The road carried him up a boulder-strewn slope
and through a narrow pass. When it began the
long descent into the valley, he paused for a minute and studied the massive encampment below.

On the steep mountainside beyond, he could see
the ancient stone amphitheater, and above that
the temples and prayer halls and teahouses of the
monastery. He hitched his pouch higher and continued into the valley.

His name was Cord, and he had been traveling
for twelve days to attend the contests. He had not
expected to find so many others, nor so many
from such distant places. But a great many of
them, he supposed, were servants and attendants
rather than contestants.

He made a broad circle around the encampment and found a small niche a short distance up
the mountainside. He gathered some twigs for a
fire, and while he ate the small bird he had cap-
tured earlier in the day, he watched the campers
below.

Some had brought drums and musical instruments, and after they had eaten they danced and
sang around their fires. Others appeared to be

9

meditating, or doing Kata exercises. When he had finished eating, Cord went down the mountainside and moved quietly among the camps, studying them from the shadows.

Each group had brought along a martial artist to compete in the contests, and most of the fighters were now practicing or doing exercises. Cord saw huge, brutal-looking men with calloused fists and necks like Braham bulls. Others were lean and hard and clearly skilled in the martial arts.

Many fighters Cord dismissed with no more than a glance. They were slow, or too heavy, or too formalized in their movements to offer any serious competition. Only three or four were impressive. One in particular: a thickly built man with muscles like bands of steel, who was practicing jump kicks, leaping high in the air and lashing out with deadly speed and strength. Cord watched him for a long time before he finally retreated to his niche.

That would be the man he would face when he reached the final contest, Cord decided. He sat down in a lotus position and thought about the man's technique. He was strong and fast, and he appeared to be a master of a broad variety of attacks and defenses. If he had any great weaknesses, they were not apparent. He was a well-oiled machine, a mechanical man whose movements were quick and precise and somewhat predictable.

Was that his weakness? Did he move in fixed patterns, always attacking or countering in predictable sequences?

Cord finally closed his eyes and breathed deeply, allowing all the impressions he had received during the day to settle slowly into his deeper consciousness. With his mind emptied, he became one with the infinite, and its strength became his. When he finally drifted into a half sleep, he was certain he would be victorious.

At daybreak, he was still meditating. In the encampment, people were donning colorful robes and preparing themselves for the day. There was less noise now, and faces were hard and determined. Cord noticed a trickle of men already moving up the mountainside to the amphitheater.

Cord frowned as he studied the scene and then turned and searched the mountainside high above him. The eerie notes of a flute seemed to be drifting down into the valley. They were low, vibrant notes at first, but then they grew richer and more insistent, as if commanding his specific attention. He studied the crevices and ridges high above the monastery, but he could see nothing. Then, like birds drifting lazily across the valley, the notes faded away.

He quickly ate what fruit was left in his pouch, and after putting on his blue robe, he followed the others up the mountain.

The ancient stone amphitheater was almost filled with spectators, who were grouped by the colored robes of their tribes. Cord moved off to the side where the contestants were gathered. A man in a cowled brown robe was seated beside a rock slab and appeared to be an official. Cord crossed the dusty area and bowed respectfully.

"I am here to participate."

The man gazed silently at him for a moment. Cord was considerably younger than the other contestants, and he did not have an entourage of attendants. "What group do you represent?" the man finally asked.

"I represent no group. Only myself."

"Your name?"

"Cord."

The man picked up a small blue stone from the rock slab and dropped it into a bowl. Cord bowed once again and moved off to the side, away from the others.

A hush fell over the amphitheater as a white-robed Elder entered the theater, followed by a group of monks. The Elder stepped up and seated himself on the dais, and the monks lined up behind him. A tall, gray-haired man stepped forward. "Morthond and Graja," he announced, breaking the silence.

Between the spectators and the Elder's dais, four judges stood at the corners of an invisible square, marking off the limits of the combat area. Two groups of men came forward, one in red robes, the other in yellow. They thrust colored pennants into the ground, and then the announced combatants stepped into the arena.

Cord smiled to himself as he watched the man named Morthond remove his yellow robe. Here was the thickly built man he had watched so closely the night before. The man's muscles rippled and bulged as he took his fighting stance. Graja, in the red robe, was heavily bearded and equally large, but he did not appear to have the strength and determination of Morthond. The two men bowed to each other, and the spectators began to chant as the referee signalled for the contest to begin.

Within the first few seconds, Cord's assessment proved to be correct. Graja lunged forward with the classical *mae-geri* front kick in an attempt to strike at Morthond's abdomen. In an instant, the leg was brushed aside as if it were an annoying fly, and Morthond struck with a front snap kick, then quickly followed with a reverse punch.

The men backed away from each other, and yellow flags were raised by two of the corner judges. Two points for Morthond. The referee quickly stepped forward, and the audience stopped chanting. The two men bowed to the referee and to each other, then reassumed their fighting stances.

With all the bowing and flag-raising, the fight was more formalized than Cord had expected. But the fighters were nonetheless talented.

Morthond's face showed nothing as he moved forward. He made a quick feint, and his opponent took the bait. The bearded man lunged into a counter side-snap-kick, but his target had disappeared. Morthond immediately scored with a solid counterpunch to the midsection, quickly followed with a controlled face punch. Once again yellow flags rose.

The referee moved between the fighters and faced the Elder on the dais, indicating Morthond to be the winner. The Elder lifted a small yellow stone and placed it in a bowl.

Morthond was very good, Cord decided. He was strong and fast and deceptive, and his concentration seemed total.

"Zolanin and Cord," the gray-haired man announced.

Cord quickly dispensed with his first opponent. The man was lean and quick, and well-trained in

13

the fundamentals, but he was a straightforward fighter. Cord easily landed a jumping side kick to the head. He scored again with an elbow strike and a driving knife hand blow to the collarbone. Within two minutes, Cord was declared the winner. He bowed to the Elder and referee and retired to the side.

As the day wore on, Cord had six more fights, and six more times he saw the Elder place his blue stone in the bowl at the side. He also had the opportunity to watch Morthond defeat five more opponents.

There was no evidence that Morthond was tiring. Nor did the big man's wooden expression change. Like a machine, he brushed aside kicks and punches, and moved steadily forward, feinting now and then, striking sharply when the opportunity came. He was fearless and aggressive, and apparently without nerves.

But Cord knew he could beat him. One way or another he would break through the man's iron defenses. He watched impatiently as Morthond battled his sixth opponent. The man was lasting longer than any of the others against Morthond. But he was doing it mostly by retreating. He moved from one side to the other and then skirted around with a jumping side kick that would fall a foot short of the mark. He was clearly afraid of Morthond.

Finally, Morthond correctly anticipated one of the kicks. As the man jumped, Morthond darted to the left, inside the kick. He struck quickly to the midsection and then the face. The man twisted in mid-air and landed squarely on his back. The yellow flags immediately went up.

14

Cord felt his heart step up a beat as the referee declared Morthond the winner and the Elder dropped the yellow stone in the side bowl. There were now only two stones in that bowl: Morthond's yellow and Cord's blue.

The defeated man came slowly to his feet and bowed to each of the judges. As he left the arena the gray-haired man stepped forward. "Morthond and Cord," he announced.

Cord pulled off his robe, took a deep breath, and moved into the arena. The spectators were silent, and he breathed deeply, composing himself. He had no supporters in the amphitheater. After each of his victories there had been a deadly quiet in the stands, and the other contestants had gazed suspiciously at him as he moved off to the side and stood by himself. Cord had paid no attention to them. He was concerned only with studying the techniques of the other fighters.

Morthond was still behind the yellow pennants, surrounded by his yellow-robed supporters. He stood perfectly still, as if in a half sleep, while they dipped rags into pots of water and sponged him off. Cord glanced at the dazzling afternoon sun and then closed his eyes, willing himself to calmness and total concentration. For six years he had been training for this moment. If he were to be the "chosen one," he must make no mistakes now.

A murmur came from the crowd and Cord opened his eyes. Morthond was moving into the arena, his face still expressionless. The big man stopped, and his dull eyes rested on Cord. Then he moved forward and assumed his fighting stance.

The crowd was chanting again, and Cord moved forward. The two men regarded each other for a moment, with Cord shifting his position slightly to the right. Then Morthond's foot flashed upward in a snap front kick.

Cord's reaction came instantly. He blocked the move and his own foot flew up in a roundhouse kick that brushed under Morthond's neck. The strike was a half-inch short of scoring a point.

Morthond retreated, and Cord moved in quickly with a cross-over side thrust kick. Morthond blocked it and counter-attacked with a spinning back kick. Cord easily evaded Morthond's move.

Cord was uncertain for a moment. He had expected his side thrust kick to score, and Morthond's block had surprised him a little. He moved warily to the side as Morthond came at him, the eyes still icy cold.

Cord made a move to attack, but quickly drew back as Morthond shifted to a counter-attack position. He feinted to the left and right, but Morthond didn't respond. Then Cord tried to surprise Morthond by snapping out a high kick and following it with a reverse thrust punch. Again Morthond was not fooled. The big man backed away from the kick and blocked the punch. Then Morthond moved to launch his favorite reverse punch. Cord saw it coming and quickly dropped back into his stance.

The chanting of the crowd was deafening now, and Morthond lashed out with a foot sweep. It missed, and Cord countered with a roundhouse kick. Neither of the strikes made contact.

Cord returned to his stance and studied Morthond. He had the feeling that a prolonged battle would not be to his advantage. Morthond's energy seemed bottomless, and there were no moves that surprised him or caught him in a position where he was not ready with a counter maneuver. The only hope seemed to be to throw all caution to the winds and hit with a storming, all-out attack.

Cord let his shoulders sag for a moment, as if to relax and re-set himself. At the same time, he took a long breath deep into the pit of his abdomen. When he released it, he yelled with all the power in his lungs, lunging forward with a leg obstruction.

Morthond's counter kick crashed harmlessly into the bottom of Cord's foot, and Cord plunged forward, his stomach taking the full power of Morthond's reverse punch.

Cord knew the punch to his stomach was a scoring strike, but he ignored it. He saw only the stolid, expressionless face, now glistening with perspiration, and completely unprotected. By instinct, Cord struck. He lashed out with a left and then a right hook, his closed fists jarring Morthond's head from one side and then the other. The big man staggered back, and Cord moved in fast, delivering another jarring hook to the face.

The crowd was roaring, and Morthond dropped heavily to the ground. But, an instant later, as Cord suddenly checked himself and stood poised over his fallen opponent, there was dead silence.

Cord knew what the silence meant. In the flurry of blows, he had used kung fu "closed fist" punches, and from the reaction of the crowd it was clear this was unacceptable. He glanced from one corner judge to the other, noting the shocked

17

looks on their faces. From the crowd of spectators behind, he could now hear the rising murmur of disapproval.

Four yellow flags went up from the corners, and Cord backed away as Morthond's yellow-robed teammates hurried into the arena. The yellow flags meant he was disqualified. Morthond would be declared the winner. Cord straightened his body and stood calmly facing the white-robed Elder.

From the moment Morthond had scored with the punch to his stomach, he had known what would happen. He should have retreated immediately and allowed the judges to raise their flags. But the temptation of Morthond's exposed head had been too great.

On the dais, the Elder gazed solemnly at Cord, his weathered face immobile. In a contemptuous gesture, he reached into the bowl and flung Cord's blue stone into the dust. The crowd roared its approval, but Cord kept his head high, showing no reaction.

Morthond was conscious now. His attendants helped him to his feet, and he moved unsteadily past Cord to a position in front of the dais.

The Elder rose and placed a leather cord with the medallion around Morthond's neck. The spectators cheered, and after a respectful bow, Morthond stumbled off to his waiting teammates.

Cord still did not move. The Elder settled himself in his chair again, and once more a hush fell over the crowd. I have two choices, Cord thought to himself. I could hang my head and shuffle away like a disgraced child—or I could boldly demand recognition. He was incapable of following the first course, and so, head high, he strode forward and stood squarely in front of the Elder. "You have made a mistake!" he announced.

The white-robed man gazed silently at him.

"You gave the medal to the wrong man," Cord said firmly.

His eyes still on Cord, the Elder reached into the bowl and lifted the yellow stone. "Is this your color?"

"No," Cord said quickly, "mine is . . ." He stepped forward, retrieved the blue stone from the dust and held it up. "This stone is mine. You dropped it in error."

The Elder's eyes darkened. "There was no error! You resorted to hard contact!"

"I won," Cord challenged.

"There are rules, and you broke them. You have been disqualified."

Cord said nothing, fighting to control himself. Under different rules he could have beaten Morthond. It should be apparent to everyone in the amphitheater that he was the better man. And that was the purpose of the contests—to choose the most competent fighter.

"Who are you?" the Elder asked. "Where do you come from that you are so uninformed?"

"My name is Cord."

"Cord," the Elder said quietly, as if tasting the word. He rose and stepped down from the dais, studying Cord more closely. "To which group do you belong, Cord?"

"To no group. I am my own man."

There were mutterings of disapproval from the spectators. Cord lowered his voice, speaking only

19

to the Elder. "I've come a long way to compete for the right to find Zetan and defeat him . . . and to see the Book he guards."

The Elder frowned. "What do you know of this . . . Book?"

"Only that it's a book . . . that it contains the wisdom of the world."

The Elder nodded. "Cord, he who is chosen to defeat Zetan must be able to bind an elephant with a spider's web, not stun it with a kick." He looked past Cord to the spectators and combatants. "Morthond has been chosen," he announced with finality.

The crowd cheered and began leaving the stands.

"Morthond is a mechanic!" Cord said loud enough for all to hear. "I am an artist!"

The Elder smiled as if amused by such a foolish statement. "Morthond has control over himself. He has cooled his fires. You, Cord, are not yet the tempered weapon that we need. Go now."

The Elder turned away, but Cord stood his ground. "One question first. Why have all the others you've sent never returned?"

The question seemed to surprise the old man. He looked sharply at Cord, then shook his head. "No one knows. Zetan has so far been invincible. . . ."

"So far . . ." Cord said with a faint smile.

"Cord, you will not go!"

Cord lifted his head and spoke loudly enough for all to hear. "I will beat this invincible man, and I will see what is in the Book!"

He turned abruptly and strode across the arena,

past Morthond, and then through the small crowd of defeated combatants.

The spectators stared after him as Cord scooped up his gear and headed down the mountain.

It was almost sunset when he reached the little niche on the mountainside where he had camped. He gathered some dry twigs, and using his flint, he started a small fire. Then he watched as the others came down the slope.

Morthond appeared to be fully recovered. His attendants were laughing and slapping him on the back, some of them giving victory yells as they scrambled down the mountain. Morthond had the same stone-faced expression, as if he were unaware of his friends' delirium. Some of the attendants spotted Cord and gave him disgusted looks as they passed. But Morthond trudged straight down the mountain, his dull black eyes showing nothing.

Some of the groups immediately struck their tents and headed out across the valley. Others prepared to spend the night, and in Morthond's camp, a big celebration began.

From his niche, Cord watched as the men danced around their big bonfire, their shouting and singing echoing through the canyons. Through it all, Morthond sat quietly in the shadows, staring off into space.

Cord was still angry. The anger was partly directed at himself for having used the closed-fist punches, and for having struck at Morthond instead of retreating. But no good martial artist would have left his head unguarded the way Morthond had. No matter what the rules, the Elder should have taken this into account, and he should have chosen the man most capable of beating Zetan. It was not likely that Zetan would respect such niceties when protecting the Book.

It appeared that Morthond was not going to start his journey in search of Zetan until morning, or some time the next day. But Cord decided not to risk missing him. He gathered his things in his hide pouch and went down the mountain.

A few of the people noticed him as he skirted the encampment, and a man shouted something in a strange language. But they did nothing, apparently satisfied that Cord was on his way home.

There was only one road leading out of the valley and into the lower mountains. Cord followed it until he reached a narrow pass between two sharply rising cliffs. If he positioned himself correctly, Morthond could not pass unnoticed. Cord moved to the side of the road and stretched out for the night.

He couldn't sleep. In his mind he reenacted every movement of his fight with Morthond, and he grew angry as he recalled the ensuing conversation with the Elder. He replayed the entire episode several times until his anger caused his heart to thud heavily against his breastbone.

He finally rose and took a lotus position at the side of the road. He must not be angry, he told himself. It is the way of the Elder and his people, and anger would not change it.

Still the disturbing events of the day intruded on his thoughts. He concentrated on breathing, drawing air slowly and steadily into the pit of his abdomen, then releasing it through his mouth. He took half a minute to complete each cycle, all the while trying to drive the turbulent thoughts from his mind.

At first the sound seemed to come from within him. It was as if his own breathing made low whistling sounds that echoed through his head. For a minute he held his breath and listened.

Not too far from him, someone was playing a flute. Cord opened his eyes and studied the darkened hills and the valley below. He could see nothing.

The notes were deep and had a rich texture, and the music was not of a kind he had heard before. At times it seemed dissonant and unmelodic. But then a sequence of notes would arrange themselves and bring the music back into harmonic balance.

Cord closed his eyes again and let the music fill his mind. Within minutes he could feel the angry thoughts gently sliding away, leaving only the clear sounds of the flute, and a delicious feeling of peace.

II

"You are a young man," Lo Tzu had said to Cord twelve days ago. Cord was preparing to leave the monastery at Djata. "You have chosen to fight for the right to seek Zetan and the Book of Wisdom. You have chosen to battle others before you have conquered yourself. You have a quick tongue and a fiery temper to fuel it," Lo Tzu had said.

"I will conquer the others, and in my victories I will be shown the way," Cord had responded.

"There will be others with similar hopes. The 'chosen one' will be neither a peacock nor a roaring lion."

"I am neither a peacock nor a roaring lion," Cord countered. "Nor am I a mouse."

Lo Tzu had closed his eyes and considered the statement for a long time. "You may go," he finally said, "and in victory or defeat, may you find wisdom."

"In victory I will be chosen to seek Zetan, and thereby find what you wish me to find."

"May it be thus," Lo Tzu had answered.

Through the years, the old monk had made many vague references to Zetan and the mysterious Book of Wisdom. When Cord questioned him, Lo Tzu had responded that Zetan was an unknown and powerful being who lived in a forbidden land, and that Cord should not concern himself with the matter. When Cord announced that he intended to find Zetan and battle him for the Book, Lo Tzu had denied permission. "Of those who have been chosen, none has ever returned," he said. "Death, perhaps, is the cost of arrogance. He who seeks to conquer Zetan is indeed presumptuous."

"Is not the avoidance of Zetan cowardice?" Cord had asked.

In the end, Lo Tzu had given Cord his blessing. But Cord now wondered if the monk had not been correct in comparing him to a peacock or a roaring lion. He had been arrogant and vain, and he had displayed a lack of self-control in his battle with Morthond. But the rules of combat laid down by the monks were foolish, and it was not surprising that none of their chosen ones had returned from battling Zetan. The monks were sending unimaginative, mechanical fighters against a foe who obviously had no regard for their foolish rules.

As he considered these questions, Cord became conscious of the warmth of the rising sun touching the side of his face. He didn't move or open his eyes. The feeling of peace was still flowing through him.

The faint *ting-ting* of a tiny bell finally intruded on his meditation. He partially opened his eyes and let the vague impressions filter through.

There were people passing, a family with three small children. The man and woman were bent forward with heavy loads, and one of the children was leading a goat. Only the children looked at him as they passed by.

The *ting-ting* was still audible, still coming closer. Cord slowly turned his head and followed the course of the road. He saw the dusty feet of a man coming toward him. The tiny bell was tied to the big toe of his foot—just visible under the hem of a light-colored robe. Cord looked up, but the blinding sun was almost directly behind the man's head. He could not make out the face.

The man passed by, walking slowly, putting little weight on his long bamboo staff. Cord felt an odd sensation, as if the man, or the staff, or the tingling bell were synchronized with the rhythms of his own body. The sensation held him for a moment, prompting his heart to beat a fraction faster. Then it faded as the man disappeared through the pass and the tingling sound died away.

Cord gazed at the empty road and then turned back to see how far the sun had risen. He shaded his eyes and squinted as another figure came into view. It was a thickly built man, moving with a heavy, resolute step.

Morthond.

Cord grabbed up his pouch and rose, quickly adjusting the shoulder strap as he waited for Morthond to reach him. Morthond's face was still expressionless, but now there were two small creases between his brows, as if he were concentrating on the difficult task before him. When he noticed Cord, the creases grew deeper. But he said nothing, and Cord heard only the rasp of deep breathing as Morthond passed by.

Cord smiled and watched the man's determined, machine-like gait. Then he stepped onto the road and began following, staying twenty paces behind.

An hour passed before Morthond looked over his shoulder. He frowned and stepped up his pace a fraction. Cord adjusted his speed to maintain the distance.

At noon, Morthond sat under a tree and ate from his leather bag. Cord did the same twenty yards away. When the big man rose and resumed his journey, Cord followed.

They moved into greener country, passing through cultivated fields of rice, and bush-like plants from which people were harvesting pendulous fruits that looked like yellow eggplants. The villages were small collections of grass huts, and the scrawny, hunchbacked people scurried away as they neared, and then gazed suspiciously at them from behind rocks and trees.

Early in the afternoon, Morthond paused at a fork in the road. One choice led into a dark forest tangled with dripping vines and thick with mushrooms and toadstools. The other switchbacked down a steep cliff and disappeared in the blanket of clouds. Morthond contemplated the two routes for only a minute, then marched down the cliff.

An hour later they were walking on damp sand.

To their right, a heavy mist hung over the ocean. They could hear the roar of waves breaking somewhere, but nothing was visible until the tumbling water came swirling gently toward their feet. To their left, high on the bluff and still lighted by sunshine, were tall masonry structures with huge bell-shaped roofs. Nearby were clusters of spherical buildings of tarnished brass and blackened silver, in the midst of which were intricate spires and what appeared to be fortresses with strange, wrought-iron symbols perched on long rods.

Along the shore adjacent to these strange cities were clusters of thatched huts, and a variety of seagoing craft—canoes, rafts, small fishing boats—drawn up on the sand, bleached and crumbling from the elements. But there was no sign of inhabitants.

Cord vaguely recalled Lo Tzu having told him about a great empire that had once flourished in the north. For several centuries, a race of giant, brown-skinned men had held the people of all the surrounding territories in slavery. In the end, they had so indulged themselves with comforts and luxuries that the whole empire had collapsed, and the people had died off from a plague.

After they had passed the cities, and the bluffs were no longer hanging over them, Morthond turned away from the coast. He followed a dry riverbed for several miles and then climbed out of it and crossed a plateau dotted with dead fruit trees. Ahead of them was a gorge spanned by an ancient aqueduct. When Morthond reached the narrow bridge, he paused as if considering the strength of the narrow stone columns. Then he headed down into the gorge.

Cord also considered the wisdom of choosing the bridge. He would have risked it if he were not following Morthond. But if he used it now, Morthond might cleverly change his course when he reached the bottom of the gorge. Cord hitched his pouch higher on his shoulder and headed down the bank.

Morthond gave a backward glance and half ran down the sandy slope. When he reached the bottom he followed the line of columns supporting the aqueduct, almost running now.

Cord paused when he reached the level ground. Morthond looked as if he had grown tired of being followed. He had probably hoped Cord would give up after the first few hours. Now it looked as if he were trying a different tactic—hoping Cord might not have the strength to keep up. Cord smiled to himself and set out at a pace that would steadily close the gap.

Morthond strode on, his arms pumping, giving Cord an occasional glance over his shoulder. Then, to Cord's surprise, the big man suddenly stopped. He stood with his back to one of the stone pillars, his dull black eyes gazing narrowly back at Cord.

After he closed the gap to the usual twenty yards, Cord also stopped. He leaned casually against a pillar and returned Morthond's gaze, showing no reaction to the changed routine.

Morthond appeared indecisive. His chest heaving, he stared off at the dry wash for a minute and then back at Cord. Then he turned abruptly and began retracing his steps, his jaw clenched tight and the furrows between his brows now deeper than ever. When he was within four paces of Cord, he stopped.

"One year ago," he said in a tight, angry voice, "I took a vow of silence."

It was as if Morthond expected Cord to bow respectfully and put an immediate end to his pursuit. Cord gave him an indifferent nod. "When did it end?"

"Now!" the man said bitterly. "Why are you following me?"

"To see where you're going."

Morthond huffed and puffed, as if close to the breaking point. "It has nothing to do with you!"

Cord smiled. "You're angry because I defeated you."

Morthond took a step forward, his face reddening. "Hard contact is forbidden! Fight me again!"

Cord pulled away from the pillar and held himself ready in case the big man charged. Morthond was too angry to fight well, and Cord half hoped he would come at him. "I never repeat my victories," Cord said contemptuously.

The man's eyes narrowed and he seemed to tremble as he glared at Cord. Instead of lunging forward, he turned abruptly and marched away. Cord moved after him, striding along almost at the man's shoulder. "Why did you take a vow of silence?"

Morthond snorted. "Follow my example," he muttered.

They climbed up the other side of the gorge, and Cord said nothing until Morthond once again settled into a monotonous pace.

"Has anyone ever defeated Zetan?" he asked.

Morthond sighed heavily. "Not yet." He glanced back, suddenly angry again. "You are still following me!"

31

"How else can I find Zetan?"

"It is not for you to find him," Morthond said. "I have been declared the winner and the most qualified. I alone am to fight Zetan!"

"But I can *defeat* him!" Cord said with innocent passion.

Morthond whirled around and glared, as if unable to believe anyone could be so foolish and persistent. Then he let out an exasperated moan and marched on.

Cord sighed and followed, once more maintaining the twenty-pace gap.

It was dusk when they reached the ruins of an ancient castle. Cord hadn't noticed it at first. For several hours they had skirted the base of some wooded foothills, passing through several villages with adobe brick homes. The people had been tall and slender and wore only loincloths. Their hair had been black and ragged and hung down below their shoulders. They seemed suspicious of strangers, and Cord noticed that they carried an assortment of treacherous-looking weapons. Several of them had paused beside the road and had eyed both Morthond and Cord, as if wondering what they might be carrying in their pouches. Then, as Morthond marched up a dry canyon and turned into another, the castle had suddenly come into view.

It appeared to have been abandoned many centuries ago. Most of the walls had crumbled, and through the years the loose stones had been used to erect temporary shelters. As they approached, Cord saw several people scamper away from an artesian well and disappear amidst the rubble.

Next to the well, a small, brackish-looking pond was buzzing with mosquitos. Morthond slowed his face and stopped, but he didn't drink. Instead he sat down heavily on a stone and turned his back to Cord.

Cord found a similar rock. He eased off his shoulder bag and watched Morthond for a while, then looked around.

On the castle walls that were still standing, streaks of a hardened black substance ran down from the notched crenelations. It appeared as if boiling oil had been poured down on warriors trying to storm the castle. He wondered how long ago the battle had taken place, and whether the attackers had been successful.

Behind the castle, the hills were all barren, as if the same invader might have salted the earth to prevent the residents from re-seeding. In the higher mountains far beyond the castle, the peaks and ridges were still laced with snow.

Cord looked at Morthond again. The man had his chin in his hands and was staring across the pond as if he were having a terrible time making up his mind what to do.

Cord looked past Morthond and frowned. About a mile ahead there appeared to be a small village. Trails of smoke were rising from the huts, and a man wearing a light-colored robe and carrying a bamboo staff was walking toward them.

Cord couldn't believe it at first. The man looked exactly like the one who had walked past him this morning. The robe was the same color, with the same peaked cowl. And then Cord heard the faint tinkling from a tiny bell.

The road curved and came up an incline. When

33

the man reached the top and moved past Morthond, Cord saw the little bell tied to the same
big toe. In his misery, Morthond paid no attention to the man.

Cord stared hard. It was the man's eyes that
caught his attention. The eyes were open, but from
the opaque, phlegm-colored balls in the sockets,
there was no doubt about his being blind.

It seemed incredible. The man never hesitated
or used the bamboo staff to feel the path in front
of him. Still, he walked with the sure-footed gait
of a man with perfect sight.

Again Cord felt an odd sensation as the man
passed. It was as if a sudden lightness overtook
him. He felt relaxed and peaceful, as if he had just
awakened from a restful sleep.

The feeling slowly dissipated as the man walked
on. He was following a different path from the one
on which Cord and Morthond had approached
the well. It angled up toward the castle, and as
the man disappeared in the rubble, Cord noticed
the faint glow of torches from somewhere deeper
in the ruins.

It was strange. There was no doubt about its
being the same man who had walked past him
early this morning. But how could a blind man
have traveled as fast as he and Morthond had?

Cord gazed at Morthond again, wondering what
the big man was going to do now that it was growing dark. Maybe he was going to sit by the pond all
night.

It seemed foolish for them to be at odds with
each other while they were both intent on defeat-
ing the same enemy. Short of beating Morthond in

34

battle again, he wondered if there was any way he could make friends with the man. Cord reached for his pouch and slipped the strap over his shoulder. Then he froze and gaped toward the castle.

At first it sounded like a man wailing some kind of high-pitched chant. But then the voice changed into an agonized scream. The scream ended with what sounded like a gurgling death rattle. Then the whole area seemed to explode with shouts and primitive war cries. Some kind of incredibly violent battle was going on.

Cord came to his feet and moved toward the sounds. Then he stopped and looked back at Morthond. The man was still slouched on his rock, still staring off into space. Would he get up and hurry away if Cord went to the castle?

Another brutal scream pierced the air, and Cord looked at the ruins again. It sounded as though at least one person had died, but the battle was still raging. He gave Morthond a final glance and loped off at full speed toward the flickering torchlight.

Cord stopped quickly as he passed the first crumbling wall. Lying on the ground was a barechested man with a broken spear protruding from the center of his breastbone. His bulging eyes were staring straight up at the sky, and his arms were outstretched, the fingers curled like claws. He was a big, hairy-faced man with large gaps between his yellowed teeth.

Cord moved past the bloody figure and along a series of crumbling arches. The light from the torches appeared to be coming from a courtyard.

He moved along the arches and then came to an abrupt stop when he saw shadows moving around in the center of the courtyard.

He was puzzled for a minute. The old man with the bamboo staff was standing perfectly still in the middle of the square, his head bowed as if in prayer. Surrounding him, but keeping their distance, were six brutal-looking men, all with weapons of one sort or another.

Six flaming torches were stuck in the ground around the perimeter of the courtyard, and at first Cord thought it was some kind of primitive ritual— with the robed man the leader. Then he realized that the man was under attack. Like wary animals, the six thugs were circling him, waiting for the right opportunity to make the kill.

Cord moved closer, at the same time keeping himself well hidden in the shadows. The assassins were a grotesque-looking lot, much like the dead man in the outer courtyard. Their clothing was nothing more than shredded animal hides, and like the other man, their heavily muscled bodies were scarred and deformed with all kinds of battle injuries. There was hate and fear and greed in their faces, and their weapons ran from heavy bludgeons and knives to rusty swords; and one man held a heavily barbed lance.

Then Cord saw the two other men back in the shadows. One was standing with his fists on his hips studiously watching the battle. From the number of animal skins draped across his shoulders, and his arrogant manner, he was probably the leader of the assassins. The other man standing to the side and just behind him was a huge, muscular brute—probably his bodyguard.

A snarling shout suddenly came from the court-yard, and one of the bigger men waved an arm, silencing the others. Then he lifted a heavy club high over his head and moved cautiously forward.

The blind man made no move, and the attacker's eyes widened as he moved closer and raised the club a few more inches.

In the silence, Cord caught his breath, then opened his mouth to scream a warning to the old man. It seemed certain that the old man's head was going to be shattered. The attacker was within three feet of him, and he brought the bludgeon down with a blood-curdling scream. But before the scream had escaped Cord's lips, the blind man was no longer there. As if the club and his body were somehow linked, the movement of one caused the movement of the other, and the blind man was suddenly standing a foot and a half to the side. At the same time, his bamboo staff whipped through a semicircle and caught the big man behind the neck, sending him sprawling into the dirt.

A second thug screamed and rushed in. Without any apparent effort, the blind man's foot whipped up and landed a deadly blow to the thug's groin. Then the blind man whirled, spring-ing away from the second man, and his other foot snapped into the head of the first man, who was just coming to his hands and knees. The man's neck snapped and he dropped lifelessly to the dirt.

The other four assassins moved instinctively for-ward, but they stopped short face to face with the blind man, who stood perfectly still. The men moved warily back, circling again, not quite as sure of themselves now.

The blind man took a short step forward and killed the second attacker with a quick crescent kick to the head. Then he retreated to his former position, once more standing as if in prayer.

Cord had never seen such a performance in the martial arts. He would never have believed it possible. From a blind man, it seemed even more incredible. He moved past two more arches and stood in the shadows directly across from the center of the courtyard.

There were four men circling the blind man now. A man with only one eye, carrying a sharp bamboo spear, waved his free arm, signalling them to stop. Then all four men crouched, preparing for a unified attack. With a snarling cry the one-eyed man signalled the charge, and all four men lunged forward, clubs swinging and weapons thrusting.

The blind man whirled in a half circle, stepping inside the one-eyed man's lance. At the same time his foot cracked the man's kneecap. Then the lance was in the blind man's hand and he plunged it into the belly of the man on his right. The lance was withdrawn as quickly as it had been thrust forward, and the backward movement plunged it into the midsection of the man preparing to club him from behind.

The one-eyed man with the shattered kneecap sidled off with a crab-like movement, screeching and gasping. The second man was dead, while the third, still impaled on the lance, was in a half upright position only because the blind man had not released the bamboo shaft. The fourth man, who had missed with the initial swing of his bludgeon, now abandoned all caution and, screaming at the top of his lungs, rushed in for the kill.

The blind man made only a small movement with his feet. He swung the bamboo shaft with its impaled victim into the path of the attacker, at the same time thrusting the lance two feet deeper through the midsection. For a moment the charge of the man with the uplifted bludgeon was blocked. Then the spear plunged through and he too was impaled. His eyes widened, the club tumbled from his grip, and both men seemed to take a half step backwards and drop to the ground.

The entire battle had taken no more than four seconds, and Cord was so awed by the performance he hadn't noticed the sudden appearance of the leader's bodyguard. Cord saw a shadow behind the blind man, and then the bodyguard was suddenly airborne, attacking the blind man with a flying side-kick.

For a moment it appeared as if the blind man, like Cord, had not been aware of the danger. But as the two impaled men dropped to the ground, the blind man took a half step forward. At the very last moment his head dropped and the bodyguard's foot sailed past, missing its target by less than an inch.

The bodyguard now spun around and faced the blind man in a classical fighting pose. The big man was superbly conditioned, and clearly an expert at empty-handed combat. As he slowly circled his opponent, the muscles of his legs and arms rippled like a mountain lion's.

Once more the blind man seemed totally at rest. But as the bodyguard circled, the blind man kept turning, his body slightly, always facing his opponent.

The bodyguard feinted to one side and then the other, but drew no response from the blind man. As if he were only mildly curious, the blind man kept his hands loosely at his side and his head slightly inclined as he turned.

The bodyguard's eyes narrowed slightly, and he moved as if to make a knife-hand strike to the collarbone. Then he swung back and charged in a reverse turning heel kick.

The blind man ducked, and Cord saw no counter blow delivered. But when the bodyguard completed his turn and whirled to face the blind man again, there was an odd look frozen on his face. Then, as if some mortal wound had finally reached his innards, his face contorted and a sick, gurgling sound came from his lips. He crumpled slowly to the ground, his entire body twitching with death spasms.

There was a faint, almost imperceptible smile on the blind man's face as he straightened and resumed his contemplative position. The man with the shatterd kneecap was still whimpering in the shadows, and the only remaining threat was the leader of the group. He had stepped forward a few paces, but it was clear that he intended to go no closer. Almost casually the leader drew a knife from his belt and hefted it, looking the blind man over, deciding on the best target. Making no sound, he gripped the knife for throwing and cocked the arm over his shoulder.

Since the moment when the first thug came at the blind man with the bludgeon, Cord had had no inclination to interfere. It was clear the blind man could take care of himself. But now, with the man poised to let the knife fly, Cord moved instinctively. His hand dropped into his leather pouch and he stepped out of the shadows, a deadly *shurken* dart in his hand.

The thug leader looked sharply back, and in that indecisive moment, Cord let out a shrieking animal cry and whipped his arm forward, letting the star-shaped disk fly. There was a flash of reflection from the torchlight, and in the same instant the six-pointed dart lodged itself squarely in the knife-thrower's forehead. The head snapped back only an inch, but the knife dropped from the man's hand as he gaped at Cord. Then, as if his body no longer had bones, the leader dropped heavily to the ground.

Cord stared at the lifeless form for a moment, then turned to the blind man, feeling pleased with himself. He searched the shadows at the other end of the courtyard. Then he turned completely around. The blind man was nowhere in sight!

He couldn't have moved away so swiftly. Or if he had, he couldn't have gone very far. Cord ran to the far end of the courtyard and ducked through the arches to the outer courtyard where he had entered. The dead man was still stretched out and gaping at the stars, but there was no one else in sight.

Cord listened for a minute, hoping to hear footsteps, or the tingling of the man's toe-bell. Other than the light gusts of wind coming up the canyons, the ruins were now completely silent.

It made no sense, Cord told himself as he walked

41

back to the courtyard. Was the man some kind of wizard who could make himself vanish and re-appear at will?

It was possible, he supposed, that the man could have gone out through the other end. But that was the direction Cord had been facing when he killed the thug leader. He would have noticed him.

The man with the shattered knee was dragging himself deeper into the ruins. He gave Cord a frightened glance and moved faster, whimpering as he disappeared in the shadows.

Cord walked around the courtyard and looked at each of the dead men. They were a scruffy-looking lot—some of them covered with lice and open sores. He removed his dart from the leader's head and returned it to his pouch.

He tripped over a battered goatskin bag. Inside were two shrivelled apples and a handful of cooked rice. Cord sighed heavily and sat down. He watched the shadows and listened for another minute, then bit into one of the apples.

He had been a fool to leave Morthond and go to the blind man's aid, he decided. All his good intentions had gotten him was a couple of rotten apples and a ball of sour rice.

He still couldn't believe it. What the blind man had done was impossible. Even a man with two good eyes would have had to be the world's greatest master of the martial arts to duplicate such a performance. And yet the blind man had never missed a target, or allowed himself to be touched. Nor did he appear to exert any energy in disposing of seven armed men.

There was another question that needed answering. Why did Cord have such a strange feeling each time the blind man walked past him? And after following—or preceding—Cord and Morthond all day, why was he coming from the village, traveling in the opposite direction? It was all very mysterious, and Cord found himself annoyed that he was not in a position to find answers. The man had distracted him from his mission to find Zetan and the Book of Wisdom. In the process, Cord had saved his life. But the man had shown no appreciation, nor had he remained to explain his actions.

Cord felt his irritation growing as he rose and walked out of the courtyard. There was no doubt in his mind that Morthond had jumped at the opportunity to escape when he headed for the castle. But there was no harm in checking.

There were two people at the well, but neither of them was Morthond. They were wrinkled old men in tattered robes, and they were tearing apart a raw chicken and stuffing it into their mouths. When they saw Cord, they turned and ran for the village, their robes flying.

Cord drank from the well-bucket and then hiked to the other side of the castle. Up the slope a short distance he found a narrow crevice from which he had a clear view of anyone approaching. He assumed the lotus position and took a deep breath. As soon as he closed his eyes he promptly fell asleep.

III

When he awakened, Cord felt dissatisfied with himself. The sky was clear, and to the east the sun was already brightening the horizon. He hooked his pouch over his shoulder and walked down to the pond, passing no other people.

After he rinsed his face and drank from the stagnant water, he gazed solemnly at his reflection. "Cord," he said, "remember what you've been taught. When looking for an answer to a question, first make sure the question *needs* answering."

He nodded, encouraged by his own wisdom. "Very reasonable," he said. "Since you can't go two ways at the same time, decide which way you can't go, and the alternative is your answer."

He nodded again. "Even more reasonable. All right. You can find Morthond and go on follow-

45

ing him. That is, if you knew where to look for him. Which you don't. Conclusion. You can't do that. The alternative?"

He nodded, knowing there was only one other choice. "Find the blind man."

He eased back on his haunches, his arms resting across his knees, and looked around the barren countryside. Was he imagining it, or was he once again hearing the deep, eerie notes of a flute? Behind him the castle ruins looked deserted. In the hills above and on the tracing of switchback trails into the higher mountains, there were no signs of life.

"Can you find the blind man?" he asked his reflection. "Do you know where *he* is? Answer: no. But the secrets you could learn from him! He sees better blind than you do with sight! What he could do to Zetan! Conclusion: the blind man."

The ponderous thumping of a drum was now coming from the village farther up the road. Cord listened to it for a minute, then followed the dusty path down the slope and into the cluster of mud huts.

Several dozen people were gathered around a central mound of dirt where a muscular black man was shouting in a strange language. His shoulders were covered with rusty chain mail, and his battered steel helmet appeared to be several sizes too small for his head. Next to him, a black dwarf was pounding a drum that was twice as large as he was.

It appeared to be an auction of some kind. Behind the black man four women stood with chains on their arms and legs. They ranged in age from

46

about fifteen to sixty, and they were wearing only burlap skirts. All of them were deeply pock-marked and appeared to be diseased or deformed in some way. Running sores covered the arms of the youngest one.

The black man's shouts sounded as if he were threatening the spectators, and an old man finally lifted a hand in reponse. The dwarf stopped pounding the drum, and the old man handed over some coins to the black man. The youngest of the women stumbled forward, and the old man grabbed her by the hair and led her off to one of the huts.

Cord waited until the auction was over and the spectators dispersed. "There was an old man here yesterday," he said to the black man. "He was carrying a bamboo staff and wearing a bell on his toe. Have you seen him?"

The black man glanced up from counting his coins, and the dwarf smiled and circled around Cord, looking him over.

"Why do you want to know?" the dwarf asked. His voice was scratchy and hollow-sounding.

Cord moved to the side and kept both men in view. "Have you seen him?" he asked.

The big man handed the coins to the dwarf, who dropped them in a pouch and tightened the drawstrings. "Of course we've seen him," the dwarf rasped. "We saw him just before the auction. How much will you pay? I'll tell you exactly where he went."

"What color robe was he wearing?" Cord asked.

The dwarf's eyes narrowed and he glanced up at the big man. "Blue," he said and smiled.

The big man grinned. "That's right. Blue."

Cord turned and walked away, heading back for the castle.

"It was an orange robe," the dwarf called after him. "I can tell you exactly where he is."

Cord didn't look back. When he reached the castle he skirted around the ruins and started up the long switchbacks toward the high mountain pass.

He walked all day, pausing only a few times to pick some berries and to rub his blistering feet. From the mountain pass the trail dropped into a broad, lava-bedded valley that had a scattering of dry brush and a few tufts of grass growing from the crevices. The sun beat down mercilessly, and the lava rock was like a sizzling grill.

He found the berries at the far end of the valley where a tiny spring bubbled down a canyon. He followed the canyon to a higher plateau that was strewn with huge granite boulders. In climbing over the boulders, the blisters on his feet were soon torn and shredded, and once he was past the rocks he limped on, the soft sand burning into his flesh with each step.

At dusk the scorching heat finally dissipated, and a spreading sheet of coolness settled over the land. Cord trudged the last half-mile to a massive outcropping of rocks and sank exhausted to the ground.

"The goal," he said with his eyes closed and his head resting on the sand, "is found in the beginning . . . the beginning contains the goal . . . the goal contains the beginning and the end. All is one . . . alertness is all."

He breathed deeply, feeling a pleasant surge of relief spread through his body. Then he was asleep.

He felt a tickling sensation in the open palm of his right hand. He opened his eyes to brilliant daylight, and then he jumped to his feet as he heard movement above him. A dislodged pebble bounced down the rocks and caromed off his head.

He was ready—feet spread, a *shurken* grasped in his palm as he searched the rocky cliff rising almost vertically above him. A bulging-eyed monkey peered down from a ledge twenty feet above. The animal scampered to a higher rock and pushed more pebbles over the side, watching them skitter down and bounce into the sand near Cord.

It was a strange-looking creature. Its body and limbs were hairy, but they were thick rather than spindly, and it had a broader forehead than most simians. It was as if the animal were half human, and it seemed to be making an effort to form distinct sounds as it squealed and banged its teeth together.

Cord returned the *shurken* to his pouch and turned away from the animal. He straightened, arching his back, and then inhaled deeply, allowing his stomach to balloon with air. As he exhaled, he sucked his abdomen deep into his rib cage. He continued the exercise for several minutes, feeling his head clear and his limbs come alive.

He relaxed for a minute, then began performing the formal *kata* exercises. His movements were precise and controlled, with each turn and kick and thrust performed in the exact manner he had been taught. A knife hand was extended and drawn back. Then a turn, a lifted knee, a foot snapped upward and quickly returned to the ground. Inhale, exhale, arm swinging through a pivot. . . .

Halfway through the exercises he suddenly stopped. For years he had gone through the same routines, but now they seemed rigid and foolish to him. The blind man didn't move by numbers! Nor was he like a tree bending in the wind. He *was* the wind!

He set himself again. He closed his eyes, remembring the man's movements, and with fixed determination he tried to duplicate them. He kicked swiftly to the left and then whirled and leaped high to deliver a head kick to a second assailant. When he completed the movements, he stood at rest, his head slightly bowed. Then he lashed out again, destroying one opponent, ducking beneath a roundhouse kick, then delivering a back kick to a man attacking from the rear.

The movements were the same, but he was not nearly as fast as the blind man. Nor could he do it in the same effortless manner. He closed his eyes and concentrated again, this time trying to empty his mind of all thoughts of technique and balance and rhythm. To fight effortlessly, he must exert no effort. He must think only of the vulnerable targets, and then allow his body to move as it wished in striking those targets. He imagined a man charging directly at him with an upraised bludgeon. Behind, another was lunging forward with a lance. A third was poised to deliver a jumping head kick.

Now! Cord told himself. He went through the

same routine, dispersing his imaginary attackers in one continuous movement of kicks and whirls.

Better. But he was still grunting and snarling, and his muscles were tense when he finished. He breathed deeply and closed his eyes, but then quickly opened them.

Was it the wind blowing through the rocks high above him? Or was it the flute again? He listened, holding his breath for a minute. Then he heard the higher notes, and the strange half-tones rising above them. It was a flute.

The monkey was gone from the cliff. He could see no other forms among the rocks. He studied the outcroppings to the left, and then looked sharply back.

The blind man stood about fifty yards to the right, almost invisible among the rocks. He was holding the long bamboo staff to his lips, and a gray bird was perched on his shoulder. Cord picked up his pouch and strode forward, watching the man closely as he picked his way among the rocks.

As Cord drew closer, the bird jumped from the man's shoulder and flapped off into the lower valley. Then a dozen more birds fluttered out of the rocks and followed along with a chorus of hysterical chirping.

When Cord was within twenty paces, the man lowered the flute from his lips and placed it on the ground. In what seemed like the same motion, his hand flicked forward and a pomegranate came flying in Cord's direction.

The man smiled faintly as Cord reached out and caught the fruit. Then he picked up a second one for himself and with one quick movement he crushed the tough-skinned fruit with the fingers of one hand.

Cord tried to duplicate the feat. Holding the pomegranate at arm's length, he squeezed with all his strength, trying to puncture the surface with his fingers. The leathery skin gave, but did not break.

Cord had not forgotten that the man was unable to see him, but he turned his back and once more pressed his fingers into the unyielding hide. Muttering angrily to himself, he finally ripped the skin loose with his teeth.

"The important thing is eating the fruit," Cord said as he moved to the blind man's side and sat down. "It's not how you get to it."

"Then eat," the blind man said quietly.

Was there a mocking tone in the man's voice? Cord couldn't be sure, but he let it pass. "My name is Cord," he said.

The blind man made no response. As if he had nothing more on his mind than enjoying the pomegranate, he continued eating, his rheumy, sightless eyes fixed on some distant point across the valley.

Cord did the same, chewing noisily, tossing bits of stripped skin off to the side. The blind man finally placed the last of his pomegranate in a bag and then sat perfectly still, his hands resting on his robed thighs.

Cord ate for another minute and finally put away a portion of the fruit. He also sat motionless.

"I'll tell you what I'm doing here," he finally said.

There wasn't a flicker of movement in the blind man's face. Cord gazed narrowly at him, then went on. "I'm looking for a great martial artist called

Zetan. When I find him, I'm going to defeat him. Have you ever heard of Zetan?"

The man still didn't stir.

"I know you're blind," Cord said irritably, "Are you deaf, too?"

As quickly as he asked the question, Cord felt a twinge of regret. He reminded himself that the man had put on the greatest display of artistic fighting he had ever seen. "I beg your pardon," he said quickly. "I was told I can't control my tongue, and now I see it is true." He looked over at the man and frowned. "There's a bee on your nose."

He expected the man to jerk his head back and slap the buzzing insect away. The man's hand flashed to his nose, but instead of striking at the bee he suddenly had it between his thumb and forefinger. He moved his hand gently to the side and opened the fingers.

Cord blinked and then gaped in disbelief as the bee flew in a broad circle and casually landed on a small wildflower a few feet down the slope.

"Who are you?" Cord asked.

The man's hand returned to his thigh and once again he became a statue.

"What's your name?" Cord asked.

The man shrugged. "Whatever you wish it to be."

"What do people call you?"

"What people?"

"Any people. What did the last person you talked to call you?"

"Do you like the name *Cord?*" the man asked after a silence.

"It is my name. I have no choice."

"With me, you have a choice."

53

"A choice of what?"

"Whatever name you wish to give me."

"Ah." Cord laughed.

"You wish to call me *Ah?*"

"No, I . . . Is that your name?"

"It is not unpleasant."

"I once knew a man named Ah Sahm."

"If it pleases you, call me that."

"The man was a thief."

"We are all thieves."

Cord shrugged. "Very well, I will call you Ah Sahm."

"Very well."

Cord studied the man, noting the strong, slender fingers and the complete repose in his erect posture. Even at rest he seemed ready to move quickly in any direction. "Be my teacher," Cord said. "Explain what you do. I want to practice it."

The man lifted his head slightly, and his voice had a faint note of disapproval. "Tie two birds together, they will not be able to fly, even though they have four wings." As if signalling that the conversation was over, the man rose and walked away.

Cord watched him pick his way unerringly between the rocks, his bamboo staff gently touching the earth. Cord finally rose and followed, staying a dozen paces behind.

"I'll just follow you and watch," he called to the blind man. "And I won't annoy you by talking. I'll just observe and learn."

Cord stumbled and caught himself, suddenly feeling clumsy and foolish as he hurried to close the gap. "I can be silent. Believe me."

The blind man moved smoothly down a zigzag

54

path and walked under a rocky archway. He seemed to be in no hurry. But he also seemed to have some destination in mind.

"They say Zetan is in possession of a book," Cord called out. "He's had it for years and years. Do you know what it is? Do you think it could be important?"

The blind man seemed to consider the question. "If a man guards a book year after year, which is more important, the man or the book?"

Cord frowned, turning the question over in his mind. If a book were extremely important, a man might certainly guard it for many years. Did that necessarily make the man important? Conversely, would an important man guard an unimportant book? He might do so if the secrets contained in the book were dangerous to his position. However, would it not be easier for him to simply destroy the book?

Cord was confused. He disliked riddles that had no clear-cut solutions.

They were walking among trees now, and Cord had to quicken his pace to keep up with the man. He hurried forward, almost trotting to reach his side.

The man suddenly stopped in a clearing and lifted his head toward the trees. Cord did the same, searching the tangled network of branches overhead.

He heard a faint chattering sound and he could see shadows darting through the foliage. Then a monkey suddenly dropped to a lower branch where it screeched and chattered, as if scolding them for entering its domain. It was the same monkey that had thrown the pebbles at Cord.

The whole forest suddenly exploded with howls and screeches, monkeys flying through the trees in every direction. The pebble-throwing monkey dropped lightly to the ground and scurried toward them.

Ah Sahm turned and his body seemed to slump a fraction as he tilted his head and listened to the soft rustling of the animal's footsteps.

The monkey moved easily, almost playfully, as it bounded forward. But there was a malicious look in its eyes as it angled warily off to the side. Then it moved in closer to Ah Sahm. The blind man slowly pivoted, continually facing the animal as it circled in one direction and then the other.

The monkey stopped and glared at the man for an instant, then tried to deceive Ah Sahm with a quick movement to the side. Once again Ah Sahm kept himself in perfect position. The monkey leaned forward and screamed at him in angry frustration. Then it scrambled away, conceding defeat.

Cord frowned, looking from the monkey to Ah Sahm. "Is that the secret? You always turn with the opponent?"

Ah Sahm was listening to the frenzied chatter overhead. "There are no secrets," he answered.

"The monkey tried to circle you, but you wouldn't let him. You kept turning. . . ."

"The way of the monkey is to play the fool," Ah Sahm said. "While you laugh at his antics, he bites you from behind. Unmask his ego . . . you expose a coward disguised as a monkey."

Cord nodded, eager to display his virtues as a student. "I'll study them. I'll watch them very carefully."

Ah Sahm nodded. "You already imitate their chattering perfectly."

Cord looked sharply at the man, suddenly annoyed by the mocking tone. It seemed that all the man had to offer was sarcasm.

"I don't have any reason to fight monkeys," Cord snorted. "This lesson has no value."

Ah Sahm listened to the monkeys a minute longer, then moved away, his voice casual and indifferent. "One is taught in accordance with one's fitness to learn."

"I have an open mind!" Cord challenged.

"Empty is not necessarily open," the man responded. He was out of the clearing and moving once more into the forest.

"I don't need you," Cord called out after him. "There must be other teachers."

"May you find one you respect," Ah Sahm chuckled.

Cord watched him disappear among the trees and then looked up at the monkeys. They were watching him from high in the foliage now, no longer chattering. Cord realized they were looking down at a fool—a man as vain and childish as they were. He sighed and hurried after the blind man.

"Wait! Forgive me!" he shouted.

He ran into another clearing, but Ah Sahm was nowhere to be seen. Cord whirled around, searching the forest in every direction. "I'll tear my tongue out and put it in my pouch!" he shouted.

There was no response. Nor could he see any movement in the trees. "Ah Sahm! I am apologizing! Can you hear me? I am sorry!"

The monkeys were silent, as if they too were listening for an answer. Then the chattering resumed. Cord looked up as the noise rose into a frenzied screeching. The animals were flying from branch to branch as if fleeing from some dangerous intruder. And then Cord heard the snapping of twigs and branches off to the side. Some kind of creature, its head down, was stumbling toward him through the thick underbrush.

Cord edged back and brought a *shurken* from his pouch. The approaching figure was human—a muscular, thickly built man who appeared to be in a drunken stupor as he reeled from side to side. The man turned as if to go back, then whirled and stumbled toward Cord again.

Cord braced himself. Then he caught his breath as the man staggered into the clearing. It was Morthond!

Cord was horrified by the man's condition. Both of his eyes had been scratched to blindness; blood still oozed down his face; his neck and back were torn with deep lacerations, and strips of raw flesh dangled from his body like bloody rags. Morthond reeled blindly forward, past Cord, and smashed into a huge rock. Then he staggered backwards and dropped heavily to the ground.

The monkeys were screeching hysterically now, and the one that had thrown pebbles at Cord suddenly dropped to the ground in front of Morthond. Eyes bulging, the little animal screamed and hissed and bared its fangs, jumping wildly up and down to taunt the wounded man.

Morthond tried to crawl away, terrified by the animal. Then he struggled to his feet and stumbled toward the forest again.

"Morthond!" Cord cried out. "Wait! It's Cord!"

The big man stopped. Then with a desperate

and pitiful look on his face, he staggered toward Cord, his arms outstretched.

Cord grabbed the bloody arms and eased the big man to the ground. Morthond dropped his head and slowly shook it from side to side.

"I have brought disgrace to my brotherhood," Morthond choked out. "I have failed."

"Zetan did this?"

"I will never find Zetan."

"Who was it?" Cord asked.

Morthond didn't seem to hear. His head was still shaking, and his voice was thick with despair. "I will never bring the Book to my brothers."

"Morthond! Answer me! How did this happen?"

He was gasping now, as if fighting for his last breath. "The First Trial," he said hoarsely.

Cord lifted the man's head in an effort to ease his breathing. "What was it? Morthond, what was the First Trial? Where?"

Morthond tried to lift a hand to point, but it shook uncontrollably and dropped back to his side. "Monkey . . ." he said.

Cord looked up at all the bared fangs and screeching lips in the surrounding trees. The hideous, nightmare faces now seemed grotesque masks on misshapen monsters—incarnations of hate and greed and evil.

"Cord," Morthond said in a hoarse whisper, "help me die."

Cord gazed silently at the man, knowing he would not last more than a minute or two. He understood what Morthond wanted: to die by his own hand rather than from the wounds of his enemies. It was the honorable way. Cord drew his

59

knife from its sheath and placed it in Morthond's hand.

The thick fingers quivered and jumped in an effort to grip the handle, but they wouldn't close.

"Cord?"

Cord leaned closer, but Morthond no longer had the strength to speak.

When a man makes a decision to die, it is important that the act be performed swiftly. Cord knew Morthond wanted help, and the silent request could not be denied.

He gently lifted Morthond into the hari-kiri position and gripped him around the back to hold him upright. With his other hand he closed Morthond's fingers around the knife and brought its point to the midsection of his abdomen.

Morthond took a deep breath, as if finally at peace. Cord then guided the hand, plunging the knife inward and through its slashing cross-tug. With its final downward pull, Morthond quietly sighed. Gently, Cord eased the big man forward to rejoin the earth. It was done.

Cord stood silently next to the inert figure, giving Morthond's soul and spirit time to depart. Then he gazed at the medallion resting in the dirt next to Morthond's cheek. He touched it, fingering the symbols, and hefted it in his hand. Then he lifted Morthond's head and slipped the medallion free. He rose and dropped it over his own neck.

Morthond had failed, and no one could question Cord's right to wear the medallion. It was now his responsibility to defeat Zetan.

There was no longer any chattering; the trees were empty. Cord glanced around and crossed to the edge of the clearing where Morthond had first appeared. With the trampled brush and broken twigs, his path was clear. Cord moved forward, glancing cautiously ahead as the trail took him through a zigzag course of underbrush.

The forest thinned, and ten minutes later Cord was in the open again. He studied the trail of bloodstains leading across a culvert and up the rise on the far side.

Directly in front of him, a quarter of a mile away, high cliffs rose sharply against the horizon. Scattered across the faces of rock were dark holes that appeared to be caves. Cord moved forward again, certain that those caves must be his destination.

IV

Once he was across the culvert, Cord again heard the low chattering of monkeys. As he drew closer to the cliffs the sound grew louder, but there were no animals in sight. At times the noise eased off. But then it would explode with a loud roar, as if some activity were exciting the animals.

At the mouth of the largest cave, he paused and listened. There was no doubt that the chattering monkeys were somewhere inside the mountain. The noise sounded hollow now, and came in resounding waves. Cord drew a deep breath and moved inside the cave.

He could see no monkeys in the dim light. Fifty feet from the entrance he came to a larger cavern with three passageways leading deeper into the mountain. The noise seemed to be coming from the one on the left, and he followed the curving, upward course.

The chattering was more distinct now, and it had a different tone from what he had heard in the clearing. The voices were deeper, and there seemed to be a ritualistic rhythm in the sound. It was almost human.

When he saw the dim reflection of light ahead, he moved more cautiously, staying close to the walls of the cavern as the roar of voices reached a deafening pitch. A moment later he found himself at the edge of a huge cavern, and he quickly hid in the shadows.

The place was packed with monkeys—most of them considerably larger than those he had seen in the trees. It was as if the others were children, and these were mature adults. They were still hairy creatures, but their faces were more human, and some of them wore clothing made from hides.

A good many of them were crowded around the outer walls of the cavern, some on the higher ledges. They were all shouting and gesticulating at two figures casually circling each other in the clearing below.

"Jungar! Jungar!" they chanted.

One of the combatants was a monkey-man— except that he appeared even more developed than the others. His brow and forehead were smooth, and he stood in an almost upright posture.

The other combatant was a man. His head was shaved, and he was considerably heavier and more muscular than his opponent. From the way he moved, he appeared to be well schooled in the martial arts. The man's three green-robed attendants, also human, stood silently to the side, as if intimidated by the incessant chanting of the monkey-man's supporters.

Cord watched for a minute, then moved to a better vantage point and glanced around the cavern. A large hole at the top of the chamber provided enough light inside so that he could see dozens of pictures and symbols carved or burnt into the rock walls. Some appeared to be ancient primitive scratchings of stick figures hunting huge unidentifiable beasts; others showed figures battling each other with clubs and spears. Still others looked like religious symbols. There were circles and triangles, huge eyes, phallic symbols, crosses, mazes, and an assortment of undecipherable hieroglyphics. Hundreds, or maybe thousands of years ago, the cave must have served as a temple or monastery.

Cord looked back at the clearing as the chanting suddenly stopped. Then it resumed at a faster tempo as the two men stopped circling and faced each other. Apparently the circling was a preliminary procedure in which they looked each other over. Now they appeared ready to fight.

The visitor made a stiff bow and touched the top of his shaved head with both hands, apparently offering his own special style of salutation. The monkey-man also bowed, but there was a derisive smile on his lips when he straightened. Then, without warning, he suddenly leaped high in the air and lashed out at the man's head with a double flying kick.

At the same instant, the surrounding monkeys screamed a battle cry, as if anticipating the move.

The other man artfully ducked both of the kicks and whirled around to charge into the monkey-man as quickly as he landed.

It was a strange fight, Cord reflected; a martial artist against a being that was half man and half beast. He wondered where the green-robed men had come from, and if they too were seeking Ze-tan.

As the two fighters dodged and feinted and circled each other, it was clear that the martial artist was trying to move in close enough to use kung fu hand techniques. But his opponent was a spinning, jumping, gyrating target, and he could no more than start a movement before the monkey was gone.

The man finally stopped his pursuit and set himself in an extended-arm pose. The monkey-man circled right, then left, then squatted low as if looking for an opening beneath the extended arms. Instead, like a suddenly released spring, he flew high in the air and lashed out with another kick. The man ducked and blocked the foot with his forearm, then came forward with a quick combination kick and knife-hand thrust. But once again the monkey-man was gone.

Cord found himself fascinated by the hairy creature's movements. The dance was exactly like the one performed by the smaller monkey when it chattered and circled around Ah Sahm. There was a strange, almost hypnotic rhythm to it that seemed to paralyze the shaven-headed man.

The man was still holding his extended-arm stance, and the monkey-man darted from one side to the other. Then, with teeth bared, the monkey-man suddenly broke the rhythm. He was weaving from side to side, and then in the next instant he was standing upright, knee lifted, and his foot snapped upward, delivering a sharp blow to the man's extended wrist.

The man's mouth opened as if to call out. Then he quickly stepped back, pulling the wrist into the fold of his stomach. He hunched his shoulders forward for a moment, then straightened and lifted his other arm.

Cord knew the man was finished. The wrist was clearly broken, and the man now had only one arm with which to defend himself.

The spectators also sensed what had happened, and their chanting rocked the cavern as the monkey-man came in for the kill. From the left side he hook-kicked to the head, and the wounded man staggered away. The monkey-man feinted to the right as if to deliver a second kick. Then, with a terrifying scream, he bounded high in the air and landed with his feet on the man's shoulders. Still screaming, he clawed viciously at the man's face and eyes, his hands now awash with blood.

Cord turned away, remembering Morthond and the hideous claw marks that shredded his face. He looked back at the dark corridor where he had entered the cavern. With the monkeys' hysterical shouting and screaming for more blood, he could easily slip through the shadows and make his way back down the passageway. He moved a few paces, then glanced once more into the clearing.

The man was down now. But the monkey-man was still screaming and gouging at him, tearing strips of flesh from his neck and back. The other monkeys were jumping up and down, shouting gleefully, demanding more. It was a sickening display of animal savagery.

Cord couldn't help picturing Morthond in the same position. A few hours earlier Morthond had stood before the monkey-man and tried to fight him in his rigid, mechanical manner. As good as he was, Morthond probably knew of no other fighting techniques. Or else he was so well trained he chose not to dishonor himself by using them. And then, with the jeering monkeys trailing him, he had staggered blindly away and somehow made his way out of the caves.

Morthond's final words echoed in Cord's head. "Help me die." And then he remembered the man's quiet courage as the knife finished him and he sank forward to the ground.

"The way of the monkey is to play the fool," Ah Sahm had said. "Unmask his ego and you expose a coward disguised as a monkey."

Ah Sahm had shown him the way, but was he capable of following it? This monkey-man was larger than the animal Ah Sahm had faced, but did that mean he was a bigger fool and coward? Or was he more human and more skilled, and far more treacherous than the little monkey in the forest?

Was this the First Trial, Cord wondered? There was no doubt about it being the place where Morthond had been so viciously mauled. And he had choked out the word *monkey* before he died.

Cord closed his eyes and breathed deeply, envisioning Ah Sahm as he stood in the clearing with the prancing monkey. Then he lifted his head and stepped from the shadows.

The screaming died as one by one the monkey faces turned to look at the tall intruder. The monkey-man finally sensed that something was wrong. He stopped clawing at his half-dead victim and looked up, studying Cord for a minute. Then he jumped from the bloody heap and stood with his hands on his hips.

The beaten man's attendants rescued what was left of their fighter, and once again the chanting resumed. The attention of all the monkey-men was now focused on Cord as he moved easily down the slope and into the clearing.

"Jungar! Jungar!" the crowd roared. The other monkeys were moving in closer now. Ten paces from the monkey-man Cord stopped and gazed evenly across the arena. He was determined not to be intimidated by the noise and the scowling, screaming faces.

There was a touch of amusement in the monkey-man's face as he came forward and looked Cord over. Cord pivoted as the man circled slowly around him.

"Where is your begging bowl?" the monkey-man asked in a booming voice.

The audience roared with laughter, but Cord kept his eyes on the monkey-man. "I am not here to beg," he said when there was silence again.

"Who are you?" the man demanded.

"My name is Cord."

The monkey-man smiled and shrugged to his audience. "If you are not here to beg . . ."

"I am here to face the First Trial," Cord said.

"Ahhh . . . he is here to face the First Trial." The monkey-man grinned at the crowd, then nodded at Cord. "Then you will beg. What sect do you come from?"

Cord kept his voice even, but loud enough for all to hear. "No sect. I come from myself."

The monkey-man stared at him in mock surprise. "A man with no mother! He comes from himself!"

The crowd laughed wildly, and the monkey-man nodded. "Perhaps you're not really a man," he said when there was quiet again. "You're a phantom. An image. What are you looking for, phantom?"

"I want to find Zetan."

"Zetan? Another phantom? And to find him, you think you have to fight Jungar. Yes?"

"Are you Jungar?"

The monkey-man laughed. "The motherless child is lost in the wilderness and does not know who he is talking to. Yes, I am Jungar. And what is your acknowledged style of fighting?"

"*My* style," Cord responded.

The monkey-man was slowly circling him again, and Cord pivoted in the manner of Ah Sahm. Except that he was suddenly conscious of his movements, and the fact that they were neither as smooth nor as effortless as Ah Sahm's. He took a deep breath trying to clear his mind, to concentrate only on his opponent.

"We have a creator here!" Jungar announced to the crowd. "He created himself, and he created his style. An interesting person. Yes?"

He finished the circle and stood once again in front of Cord. Cord breathed more easily, keeping himself relaxed.

70

"Listen to me, self-created man," Jungar said. "Go back the way you came." He smiled and gestured toward the corridor. "In peace."

The knowledge that he might soon be dead seemed to have a calming effect on Cord. Neither the crowd nor Jungar's game of ridicule rattled him.

"I don't want to go back," Cord said quietly. "And I don't want to fight you—unless I have to, to find Zetan."

Hah!" Jungar snorted. "Here we have Zetan again. Babies don't look for Zetan. Especially motherless babies. Go back where you came from, motherless one."

The others laughed, but Cord remained silent, his eyes resting coldly on the monkey-man.

"Zetan is far away," Jungar said. "On the other side of me. To reach him—you must pass through me."

"What if I just walk around you?"

Jungar regarded him silently, then slowly shook his head. "But that is not in the order of things. Yes? If I am a trial, I am a trial. You cannot walk around it."

"Then I will have to pass through it. I will have to fight you." Cord shrugged, mimicking the monkey-man. "Yes?"

"Yes," Jungar said, as if pleased by the joke. "You will have to fight me, motherless one."

The others backed away now, once again resuming their chant as Cord and the monkey-man took positions facing each other.

The men in the green robes had carried their wounded fighter up the slope to the exit corridor.

71

They had no interest in watching another slaughter, and they continued on their way, disappearing in the darkness.

Jungar bowed in the same style as he had to his previous opponent. Cord gave him a brief nod. He saw no point in observing formalities with a man who fought so crudely.

Cord held himself easy, ready to counter if the man jumped into the same quick double kick he had used on the other opponent. Instead, Jungar darted forward with a front kick that was far short of the mark. He spun and side-kicked, then leaped high in the air and went through the motions of a jumping front kick. Cord hardly moved, pivoting only slightly to keep the man in front of him.

Jungar was not fighting. All his jumps and twirls and gyrations were a dazzling performance designed to hypnotize Cord. None of the kicks or punches came anywhere near the mark, and he screamed and chattered and contorted his face as he danced and feinted around the perimeter of the clearing.

Cord waited, slowly pivoting, keeping his mind clear and his attention focused on the task before him. Within the insane movements and hypnotic patterns was a deadly enemy, and at any instant a hand or a foot could lash out with a lethal strike.

It came two minutes later. Jungar circled faster and faster and began feigning attacks. He moved in closer for an instant, and a foot whipped past within inches of Cord's head. Then a knife-hand thrust darted out and was pulled away, and Jungar was feigning a groin attack with a kick

72

that fell short. When he finally came in all the way, it was with a lunging forefist strike aimed at the chin.

Cord was ready. His left arm knocked the driving fist to the side, and with the same motion he brought his right foot up and ground it into Jungar's abdomen just under the breastbone.

The frenzied rhythm of Jungar's dance and the spectators' chanting were suddenly broken. Jungar backed away as if both surprised and stunned by the blow.

Cord showed no emotion. He returned to his stance and breathed easily, ready for the monkey-man's next move. He felt confident now, and far more relaxed.

Jungar went into his gyrations again, but they seemed less energetic than before. He kicked and twirled and completed another circle around Cord. Then he stopped and frowned, as if uncertain what to do next. Still holding his stance, Cord gazed evenly at him.

The chanting had now turned into a mixture of angry screams and snarls, and the monkey-man no longer seemed to have his simian characteristics. He moved uneasily from one side to the other, glaring at Cord, taking one stance and then another. He had the look of a man who wished he had never become involved.

Screaming maniacally, he finally rushed forward in a violent, reckless lunge, his technique no longer smooth. The clawed hands were grasping and trying to fight their way through Cord's defenses.

It was now Cord's kind of fight. The only thing in the man's head was blind rage, and he was going for Cord's throat with no thought of defending himself. Cord quickly shifted to the side, at the same time smashing a fist into the man's nose. His other fist drove into the abdomen, penetrating deeply with a last-second twist of the wrist.

Jungar grunted from the almost simultaneous blows. His hand went quickly to his face, leaving his midsection unprotected. Cord moved quickly forward and drove his knee squarely into the man's groin. He followed with a sharp knife-hand thrust to the throat.

Jungar was finished. As if his lower abdomen had been struck by a cannonball, he doubled forward with a soundless cry. Then his legs gave out, and he crumpled to the ground.

Cord moved forward again, ready to snap the man's neck with a short front kick. Then he hesitated, watching Jungar writhe in pain. He remembered Ah Sahm, and the way he had stood composed and silent among the thugs in the castle ruins. Cord finally stepped back and gazed coldly at the surrounding spectators.

They were no longer chanting. There was anger and resentment and surprise in the grotesque faces. But none of them made a move to attack.

Jungar finally managed to get to his hands and knees. But he continued to gasp for breath, his eyes fixed on the ground. Blood oozed freely from his nose and mouth, and he quietly spat two teeth into the dirt. He reached up and lightly touched his mouth, then looked at the bloody fingers.

"Now tell me the way to Zetan," Cord said.

Jungar closed his eyes and took a long, recovering breath. When he rose, a faint smile came to his face. He touched the gap where his two front teeth had been shorn away, then wiped the fingers on the fur of his loincloth. "There are as many ways as there are seekers." he said and ran his tongue over the bleeding gums.

"*My* way," Cord said.

Jungar considered for a minute, then lifted an arm. "Let the west wind embrace you. Until you you come to a wilderness. Look for a rose there."

Cord gave him a narrow look, wondering if there was any reason to trust the man. "Look for a rose? Is that the Second Trial?"

The other monkey-men were watching in respectful silence. Jungar shrugged, apparently making no further attempt to entertain his supporters. "You asked the way to Zetan."

"Are there others ahead of me?" Cord asked.

Jungar shook his head. "No. You are the first to pass me. But perhaps other seekers have other trials."

"I understand."

Cord crossed to the edge of the clearing where he had dropped his pouch. When he returned, he smiled at Jungar. "Am I a beggar with a begging bowl?" he asked. "I have now put you in my bowl, Jungar."

The monkey-man sucked at his bleeding gums and nodded. "You will need a very large bowl before you find what you are looking for, Cord."

Cord laughed, and the monkey-man gestured sharply at the others, commanding them to let Cord pass. The crowd edged back, some of them still grumbling, and Cord strode past.

When he reached the end of the passageway and came out into the late afternoon sunlight, he paused and looked toward the valley. The three men in the green robes had improvised a stretcher and were carrying their fighter off toward the forest where Morthond had died.

Cord wondered what kind of contests the man had won to earn the right to look for Zetan. He also wondered about the "other seekers," and the trials they were undergoing. Were there many of them? And would they be required to battle each other before they faced Zetan?

He smiled as he adjusted his pouch and headed away from the setting sun. With Ah Sahm's help he had easily passed the First Trial. He had proved himself now, and no one could question his right to wear the medallion he had taken from Morthond. He felt free and strong, and he had no doubts about conquering Zetan and taking possession of the Book of Wisdom.

V

"Let the west wind embrace you. Until you come to a wilderness. Look for a rose there."

The words puzzled Cord. Letting himself be embraced by the west wind was clear enough. He should travel east. A wilderness, on the other hand, could mean anything—a forest, a jungle, a desert.

As he traveled he watched for foliage that might contain a rosebush with flowers. Yet he knew "the rose" might not be a flower. It could be something fragrant, or delicate, or even thorny.

He slept by a brook in a deep forest the first night. The next day he came upon a surging river and was forced to travel several miles upstream before he could swim across. Once on the other side, high mountains blocked his path, and it was dark before he stumbled down the slopes on the eastern side.

He was not certain, but several times along the way he thought he heard Ah Sahm's flute. The first was when he plunged into the river and fought through the raging current. Then, when he reached the thin air of the mountain pass and sat down to rest, the eerie notes once again seemed to drift by with the gusts of wind. The hollow tones would be distinct for a moment. Then, just as quickly, the wind would shift or disappear and the entire mountain range would be engulfed in empty silence.

On the second morning, while he was meditating and then doing his exercises, he heard the notes again. They were higher now, and seemed to be beckoning him to the east. When he resumed his journey, the flute sounds again disappeared.

The morning sun was blinding, and within an hour Cord found himself descending rocky, desert-like slopes into what appeared to be an endless dry lake. On the slopes, cactus and spear-like plants were growing between the blistering rocks. But once he reached the bottom there was nothing but miles and miles of sand dunes.

He rested awhile, wondering if he should skirt the vast wasteland by following the edge of the dry hills. But it would make his journey half again as long, and he was no more likely to find water in the hills than he was in the desert. He finally took his bearings and struck out directly eastward, plodding steadily over the heat-scorched dunes.

An hour later the dunes ended, and a flat expanse of dry, cracked mud stretched out for miles in front of him. Cord gazed at the heat-blurred horizon for several minutes and then trudged on.

He wondered if Jungar, with all his black humor, might have played the final joke on him. No doubt the monkey-man was aware of the empty wasteland lying to the east. And if there was a rose anywhere within it, Cord could not imagine it anywhere within the next fifty miles.

The sun was directly overhead, and the gray-brown clay seemed to sizzle and penetrate his feet as if it was the glowing hot surface of a cooking skillet. He breathed deeply and tried to ignore the pain by concentrating on the hazy line of mountains twenty miles ahead. Each step was taking him closer, and with each passing minute the sun was moving an inch farther to the west.

An hour later Cord blinked and wiped the perspiration from his eyes. He was certain that the odd-looking form a half-mile ahead of him was a mirage. It looked like a dead tree with a dark shape resting at its base. When he blinked, the whole thing blurred and seemed to jump in all directions. Then it settled down again, and its outline seemed even more distinct.

Cord shook his head and trudged on for a few more minutes before he squinted at the form again. It was still there. And now he could make out the shape of a man standing under the tree. He could see the head and shoulders and the two arms. Below that there appeared to be a barrel. Cord stopped and studied the figure for a minute, then continued walking. This desolate expanse of baked mud could probably qualify as a wilderness. But the man bore no resemblance to a rose.

When he was ten paces away, Cord stopped again. Now he could clearly see that the man was standing in a barrel or cask of some sort. The thing was made of brass with large handles around its sides, and rose almost to the man's armpits. The man was partially bald, and looked to be about fifty years old. His eyes were closed; his arms rested on the top edge of the barrel.

It was a ridiculous sight. Cord turned and looked in every direction, wondering where the man might have come from. There wasn't another stick or stone or sign of life within ten miles. He moved forward again to a position directly in front of the man.

The man didn't move or flicker an eyelid. Inside the barrel, and rising to the level of the man's waist, was some kind of clear oil. Cord looked at it —then blinked with surprise and revulsion. The man no longer had any legs. Or at least what was left of them was nothing more than shriveled strands of flesh hanging onto the bones like pieces of seaweed. Cord stared at the man's face, and the two enormous eyes suddenly popped open. There seemed to be no concern in the man's expression—he might have been standing on a road somewhere, watching people pass by.

"Can I help you?" Cord asked.

"Help me?" the man said as if surprised. "Help me do what?"

"To get out of the barrel."

"Why?"

Cord frowned and looked in the barrel again. He had not been mistaken; the flesh was almost gone from the man's legs, and what remained was rotten and disintegrating. "Who is torturing you this way?"

The man gave him a puzzled look. "Torturing me what way?"

Cord wondered for a minute if he was heat-struck and hallucinating. But the man and the barrel were certainly real.

"Who put you in there? Isn't that barrel full of oil?"

"Of course. I filled it myself."

"*You* did it?"

The man nodded. "I filled it myself, and I got in it myself. I've been in it for ten years."

"But . . . why?"

"To rid myself of the bottom half of me." The man edged back and peered into the barrel. "There's very little left now."

Cord nodded. "Your legs look like seaweed."

The man sighed. "I hope so. And that thing, that terrible thing between my legs. It's almost gone now, isn't it?"

Cord glanced in the barrel again, finding the sight even more repulsive now. "Yes, it's almost gone. It's a mere pimple."

"Good. Soon it'll go altogether. I hope."

Cord looked at the tree behind the man. It was no more than a gray trunk and three or four branches, dried out and parched by the desert heat.

"Ten years," Cord said. "How do you live without eating?"

The man shrugged. "My family brings me a little rice, a little water."

"Your family? They . . . they *know* you're dissolving yourself in oil?"

"Yes. They weren't too happy about it to begin with. Especially my wife. Now she understands."

"Understands what?"

"That it's the only way. To rid myself of the terrible needs of that . . . that pimple."

"But why would you want—" Cord suddenly realized what the man must have had in mind. Apparently he had aspirations to improve himself and achieve some higher spiritual level. "You could have taken a vow of chastity," Cord said, "as I have done."

The man laughed bitterly and shook his head. "Oh, I took a vow of chastity, all right. I took ten vows. A hundred. But that terrible thing wouldn't let me rest. Day and night it tortured me. How can a man be a holy man when that terrible thing attaches him to earthly pleasures?"

Cord shook his head, too amazed to argue.

The man looked up at the sky and sighed. "I got rid of my money. I shed my clothes, I ate only a spoonful of rice a day, and my mind soared. I could feel the universe. I *was* the universe!" He dropped his head and frowned at Cord. "You know what happened?"

"No," Cord said.

The man's eyes widened. "That terrible thing summoned me! 'Hello,' it cried. 'Think of the pleasure! Think of the joy and satisfaction; the wonderfully sensual experience of physical catharsis!'" He shook his head and tears suddenly glistened in his eyes. "Several times . . . several times I grabbed a knife and intended to rid myself of it once and for all. But I was . . . a coward. I couldn't do it."

82

Cord stared at the man, not knowing what to say. He was clearly crazy.

"But then," the man said, suddenly smiling, "I saw the way! I would stand in a barrel of oil and dissolve it away. And the legs that carried it along."

Cord had never seen anything so ridiculous, or heard anything so stupid. "You were obviously mentally disturbed," he said. "You should have seen a doctor."

"I am a doctor!" The man smiled. Then his eyes narrowed as he studied Cord. "You say you took a vow of chastity?"

"Yes."

The man shook his head. "You won't keep it!" He edged to the side of the barrel. "Come in here with me."

Cord quickly backed away as the man reached out a hand.

"Come on," the man said. "There's plenty of room. We'll keep each other company!"

Cord moved around the barrel, staying well out of the man's reach. "I'm sorry, but I must go. I'm looking for someone."

"Who?"

"Zetan."

"Again Zetan!" The man sighed and shook his head. "They all come by looking for Zetan. There is no answer in Zetan. Believe me, the answer's in here with me!"

Cord started moving away. He was past the barrel and the tree now, and he struck out once more across the empty desert. Behind him he could hear the man thrashing violently in the oil.

"If you won't melt it off, cut it off!" the man cried out to Cord. "Whatever your dreams are, it will ruin them! It's like a sword, that terrible thing! You must get rid of it. It will cut you to death!"

Cord began loping across the hard clay. The man's strident voice seemed to ring in his ears, and he ran faster, racing at full speed toward the distant hills.

When he was at least a half-mile away, he finally eased his pace to a slow jog and then came to a stop. The man was still shrieking, but now his voice was only a faint squeak in the empty desert. Cord gazed back at the blurry figure, and finally smiled.

The more he thought about it, the funnier it seemed. Ten years! It was incredible. Then the whole incident struck him as hilarious, and he dropped to the ground laughing—brought on partly by exhaustion.

"It you won't melt it off, cut it off! Do it now!" He could still see the urgent, desperate look on the poor man's face. And he was a doctor!

Cord finally emptied himself of laughter. Breathing heavily, he lay on the hot clay for several minutes and squinted up at the blinding white sky.

In the monastery Lo Tzu had often talked about chastity, and the perils of unchecked wantonness. The desire for women, he said, is a fire-breathing dragon that must be slain before a man can ascend into the temple of wisdom. Cord had always listened, but he had never given much thought to the words. Before his vow of chastity, he had been intimate with many women. In the villages there were many willing women. But he had never found the need compelling enough to interfere with his other disciplines. It was only because of Lo Tzu's fears that he had taken the vow. If he was to find and conquer Zetan, Lo Tzu told him, he must show total dedication.

Cord smiled, wondering how Lo Tzu would have reacted to the man in the barrel. He would have been shocked, and he certainly would not have approved. A man who has never come into contact with alcohol cannot be admired for abstention, he often said. It would follow that a man without genitals could hardly claim a victory over lust and wantonness.

Cord finally pulled himself to a sitting position and looked once more toward the man in the barrel. The heat-wave distortions made the man almost invisible, but Cord could still hear a faint moaning and wailing from that direction. He listened for a minute and then looked the other way, suddenly puzzled.

The sounds were not coming from the man. They were flute sounds. Cord listened more closely, then came abruptly to his feet and looked around.

There was not a soul in sight. The desert was empty, and except for a single gust of wind that swept past, there was now complete silence.

The gust of wind had come from the direction of the man in the barrel. Cord watched it swirl off toward the other horizon, lifting small clouds of dust and whipping them through miniature whirlwinds. He finally picked up his pouch, slung it over his shoulder, and moved on.

More gusts of wind whipped past him as he walked. They seemed to be urging him along, and he soon found himself trotting as the wind buffeted him faster. He increased his speed until he was loping at almost full speed. The fast pace required little effort; at times it seemed that his feet hardly touched the ground. The wind was like a tonic. It brought relief from the intense heat, and it carried him buoyantly along as if he were a feathery tumbleweed. He grinned and ran faster, watching the earth race beneath him as if he were on a treadmill.

At last he came to the end of the parched mud. Through the final hundred yards, he had slowly eased his pace. Then he dropped into the warm cushion of a broad sand dune. He was now completely out of breath and exhausted, but he also felt exhilarated.

As he lay panting in the late afternoon sun he felt completely at peace. He was well satisfied with the last few days. He had beaten Jungar and passed the First Trial, and he had crossed a broiling desert without a drop of drinking water.

His legs felt like numbed stumps when he finally rolled to his hands and knees and looked around. A short distance past the sand dunes, some dry hills led to what appeared to be a higher plateau. The canyons to the left had faint splotches of green where they emptied into the basin.

His legs were shaky and hard to control when he finally rose. Before the muscles could tighten and cramp, he started walking, once more moving into a steady rhythm.

It was almost dark when he reached the mouth of the canyon. The green splotches turned out to be a few gnarled poplar trees standing along the banks of a dry wash. Higher in the canyon he could see nothing but rocks and a few cactus plants. He moved on, following the contour of the foothills along the desert floor until he reached the next canyon.

This canyon was also barren and dry. With dusk fast approaching, he pushed onward, around the next hill and up the broad, sandy wash into the next canyon. There were no green leaves, nor any other evidence of water, but he continued up the narrowing gorge. For some reason he was certain there was water there. He sensed it, as an animal might.

There were great overhangings of rock, almost turning the canyon into a cave. In the darkness, Cord stumbled onward, scraping his feet and bare legs on rocks and dead brush. Then, feeling his way, he came to an abrupt stop as his fingers touched a cold slab of granite.

He felt the rough surface with both hands, moving one way and then the other. Close to the ground he could feel moisture. He crawled forward into what seemed like a shallow cave, and his hand finally touched moss and damp earth. He quickly dug into it, patting the moist earth onto his arms and legs.

When the hole was a foot deep, he broadened it and gently patted the sides, drawing the moisture to the surface. A small puddle finally formed at the bottom, and he lowered his face into the hole and gently sucked in the cool, muddy liquid. He continued the operation until his thirst was finally slaked. Then he dropped heavily to the ground and slept.

If a man had the Book of Wisdom in his possession, he would be the wisest of men. It would follow that the wisest man would also be the most powerful. Thus such a man could easily defend himself against anyone who sought to take the Book away from him.

How did Zetan get the Book in the first place? And who wrote the Book, and when? And in what language was it written?

Cord pondered these questions as he made his way down the canyon the next morning. He also wondered whether Zetan devised the trials for those aspiring to reach him. Were they really trials, or were they merely designed to protect his domain from intruders? Would not a wise man—the wisest man in the world—devise such a scheme? He would certainly use every device and subterfuge to prevent seekers from reaching him.

It didn't matter, Cord reflected. Whether they were trials or Zetan's outposts of defense, he would surmount them all.

The sun had just risen above the eastern horizon, but it was already a disk of fiery white heat that was scorching the hills and the desert below. Cord stood on a high rock and shaded his eyes to study the route he must take. Directly to the east was another endless stretch of sand dunes and alkaline basins, all of it shimmering in the morning heat.

He climbed down from the rock and then froze for a minute, watching a speckled lizard make intermittent dashes across the sand below him. The creature finally scampered up the side of a rock and perched on the top, its belly puffing in and out.

Cord moved slowly, keeping directly to the rear of the reptile. When he was within striking distance he lunged forward and grasped it around the shoulders, keeping its head straight with his thumb and forefinger. He killed it with a quick snap of the neck, and carried it down to the bottom of the hill.

He had never eaten lizard meat, and the thought of it turned his stomach a little queasy. But the taste turned out to be much like chicken. Once he managed to swallow the first bite he ravenously devoured every morsel. His hunger sated, he hitched his bag on his shoulder and resumed his trek.

The heat seemed more intense than during the previous day. Through most of the morning he traveled across a flat wasteland of alkali dust that clogged his nostrils and settled thickly in his throat. What little moisture was in his body was leached away by the chalky material. By noon his eyes were parched and red-rimmed, and he no longer was able to produce tears. He finally decided to keep them shut, and tried to sense his direction by the searing heat across his back.

When the sand dunes finally appeared, he burrowed deeply into the first one in search of moisture. There was none, and with his lips now cracking and his throat and nostrils caked and dry, he rose and trudged forward. By mid-afternoon it was clear that he would not make it across the desert before nightfall. To save what little energy he had left, he dug a low trench on the eastern side of a sand dune and there he slept, protected from the slanting rays of the sun's heat.

When the sun finally touched the western horizon, he forced himself to rise and continue walking. His legs were now brittle and his feet seemed to flop numbly as he climbed dunes and stumbled down the other sides. But once again the wind was rising, and it seemed to nudge him along.

When darkness came, he was still moving—the eastern star ahead of him and the north star to his left. The wind was blowing harder now, and the swirling grains of sand tore painfully into his back. But he could no longer feel the earth under his feet. His legs were like two blunt-ended stumps that flopped alternately forward. He staggered to the crest of a sand dune and reeled and slid down the other side. Then up and down another, and then another. He opened his eyes and squinted only at brief intervals.

Finally, his legs would no longer respond to the thudding, methodical rhythm that echoed through his head. From the crest of a dune, one step fell short. The next reached out in an effort to regain the lost balance, and then he was skidding headlong down the slope.

For several minutes he did not move. He lay with his head buried in his arms while the wind howled and tore sand from the crests of the dunes above him. He finally rose to his hands and knees and breathed deeply, trying to gather some strength. But his arms and legs quivered and he was unable to rise. Above him, the blowing sand was so thick he could no longer see the stars.

He dug with one hand and then the other into the hot sand, but he managed to produce no more than a shallow groove. He crawled into it, covered his head with his arms, and closed his eyes.

In his exhaustion and dehydration, he realized that he was nearly delirious. Above the raging howl of the wind he could hear the tinkling of bells and the jangle of tambourine cymbals. He stopped breathing for a minute and listened more closely, but the sounds quickly disappeared. Then, with his rasping breath, they came back again. He covered his head, knowing the bell sounds must be inside his own chest.

In the morning the wind was still blowing. But now it was a steady gale that filled the air with a fine mist. Cord lifted himself from the mound of sand that had accumulated over him.

His bones ached, his lips were crusted and cracked, and his skin felt like tautly stretched leather. But miraculously, he seemed to have at least partially replenished his store of energy. He climbed to the top of the dune and once more looked to the east.

The sun was a dull orange disk through the haze of blowing sand. Below it, he could make out the faint outline of a mountain range. How far was it? Twenty miles? Thirty? He took a deep breath and strode down the dune and up the next one. Surprisingly his legs felt even stronger than the previous morning. He moved up and down the dunes with long, even strides, once more falling into a steady rhythm.

Was he still delirious, he wondered? He smiled at the thought, but decided not to question it too closely. If his delirium helped him to keep up a good pace, he didn't want to bring himself back to reality.

He thought about Ah Sahm, wondering where

the man had gone. Had he gone off in some other direction—to the west, maybe—expecting Cord to follow? Or would he magically appear on the desert with more sarcastic words of wisdom? Cord was not sure he would be as respectful the next time he saw the man.

By noon the wind had died and he stopped to rest. The mountains were closer now, but they were still no more than low, hazy forms on the horizon. After fifteen minutes, he rose shakily to his feet and forced himself into the same fast pace he had maintained through the morning.

At dusk he was still moving, but he was hardly conscious of it. For hours he had plodded on, his mind a blank and his eyes fixed numbly on one slope and then the next. When the sun was almost down he had lifted his head and blinked at the distant mountains for several minutes. He could not make it, he realized. He would have to spend one more night in the desert. Dimly he questioned whether or not he would survive that long without water. But it was not a matter to worry about. He would sleep soon. He would lie down between two sand dunes, and he would either wake up in the morning, or he would not.

VI

Tinkling bells. He was hearing them again as the air scraped in and out of his throat. The bells were rhythmic, and tambourine-cymbals sounded intermittently. But neither sounds were in the same rhythm as his breathing. Odd.

He could go no farther. Legs quivering, he thudded down the slope of a final sand dune and dropped to his hands and knees. For several minutes he breathes deeply, his head hanging between his arms. Then he eased himself into a sitting position and squinted at the stars.

The bells and cymbals were both tinkling now. Once again he held his breath and listened. This time the sounds did not stop. He was certain his mind was not playing tricks on him. Was it Ah Sahm again? That was impossible! Cord hauled himself wearily to his feet and climbed the next sand dune.

Laughter now mixed with the other sounds. At the top of the dune, he turned a complete circle, studying the desert in every direction. Then he blinked, not trusting his eyes as he squinted off to the northwest.

The sand dunes rose and dropped off about a quarter of a mile away. Beyond the mound he could see three small, triangular flags that looked as though they were flying from the tops of broadly spaced tents. Was it possible? Or was he hallucinating?

He ran, stumbling down the first sand dune, then struggled up the next. The flags were still there. He continued over the dunes, steadily rising higher on the mound.

An incredible sight met his eyes when he finally reached the top. There were tents—dozens of them! And people! It was a huge desert encampment spread across a quarter-mile of sand dunes.

Cord was suddenly conscious of his swollen tongue, cracked lips, and parched lungs as he stumbled down the dunes. It was not a mirage. As he crested each small dune the tents grew larger and the bells and cymbals and laughing voices were louder. There were campfires and torches, and he could see crowds of people everywhere in the camp.

When he had heard the bells the night before, had the caravan been camped nearby? How could he possible have missed it? Or had the caravan traveled during the night while he was sleeping?

When he was within fifty yards of the closest tent, Cord came to a halt and studied the encampment more closely. Several guards were spaced along the perimeter. They were big men with weapons, but they seemed to be more interested in the activities in the camp than watching for intruders. Two of them were talking to scantily clad women; and onther was laughing and drinking from a wineskin.

There were camels tethered off to the side, and what looked like concubines and slave girls were laughing and dancing, going from tent to tent. Servants with silver trays were delivering food, and there were even clowns and magicians and sword swallowers entertaining the crowds.

Cord was puzzled. He had expected to see only the dark faces of Arabs in the encampment. But the people appeared to be from every race on earth. There were Orientals, Africans, Caucasians, Arabs—and a good many who appeared to be combinations of many races. It reminded him of the encampment at the monastery where he had fought Morthond. Except that the people here seemed to be having a gigantic party.

The smell of food cooking over the fires brought a deep ache to Cord's stomach. Even more tantalizing was the certainty that there must be plenty of water in the camp. But would they welcome him?

Cord moved to a position midway between two of the guards before he straightened and marched forward. One of the men turned and looked squarely at him, and he held his breath as he continued walking. But the man showed no particular interest. He turned away, and the girl beside him popped a morsel of food into his mouth. Cord kept moving and glanced to the other side. To his surprise, the guard with the wineskin was smiling at him, almost as if welcoming him to the camp.

The tents seemed to be arranged in no particular pattern. The open areas between them looked like bazaars, complete with merchants' stands, jugglers, naked women of all colors, musicians, dancers. . . .

Cord looked around, his gaze finally resting on a small unattended tent with baskets of fruit piled in front. On the posts supporting the open flap were bunches of grapes, and a dripping goatskin. He glanced in both directions, then strode across and lifted the goatskin to his mouth.

The water was clean and pure, and deliciously cool in his dust-caked throat. When his stomach was filled, he let the rest of the water pour over his head and face and stream down his chest. When the skin was empty he grasped the pole and closed his eyes for a minute, feeling the precious liquid slowly spread through his body.

Nobody seemed to be watching him. He returned the skin to the post and detached a bunch of grapes as he moved back into the crowd.

He still wondered if he had walked into a mirage. As he moved along he stared at the colorfully dressed people and the mounds of food, and then he stopped short when he reached a small open area.

A man and a woman, both naked, were locked in a writhing embrace in front of a tent—both shrieking and gasping as if at the point of climax. No one was paying any attention to them. Others were drinking from huge flagons, or smoking hashish, or dragging giggling girls into tents. Cord stared as an Oriental girl rolled back on a Persian rug and held her bared legs and torso high in the air. A Caucasian girl wearing nothing more than an open robe joined her. The two of them became entangled; giggling and squirming, tumbling back and forth across the rug. Cord finally turned and moved on.

Musicians were everywhere; fiddlers, sitar players, flutes, ocarinas, and instruments Cord had never seen before. Dwarfs, hunchbacks, cripples, people on stilts, women wearing gypsy skirts and gold earrings, others in tights, G-strings, brocaded gowns; strong-men, men in silk loincloths, leotards; a one-eyed man wearing a wig and a woman's underclothes; a man with a turban and a huge scimitar through his belt. It was a circus, a bazaar, and a bacchanal all wrapped into one.

Cord grabbed a passing arm and found himself staring at a naked man carrying a roasted chicken. "What is this place?" he asked, "What's going on? Who runs this place?"

The man gave him only a glance, then bit into his chicken and walked on.

Cord moved deeper into the encampment, finding the same frenzy of activity. In the center was a huge velvet tent spread over a half-acre of ground. Low couches and silk cushions were scattered over richly carpeted floors, and the thick, musty smell of incense drifted from the opened doors.

Cord stopped another man—a tall Arab wearing a striped djellabah and a dozen jewelled rings on his fingers. "Is there an owner here?" he asked. "A ruler? Are there trials in this place?"

Either the man didn't understand Cord's language, or thought he was crazy. He frowned for a minute, then drew his arm away and marched off.

Off to the side of the velvet tent, a big Turk

with hair flowing to his shoulders was massaging the back of a huge black bull. Cord watched him, realizing he was the only man in the entire encampment who seemed to be doing anything other than indulging himself. Cord moved past the tent to the man's side.

The Turk was working on the bull's shoulders now, kneading and pounding them. The animal's head was lowered, its eyes closed, snorting with pleasure.

"I can see everyone is too busy to talk to me," Cord said, "But if you could spare me . . ."

The Turk turned away and wiped his hands on a scrap of towel. Then he gave Cord a brief smile and walked away.

Cord wondered if nobody understood his language. Or was everybody in the place intoxicated with drugs and alcohol? He suddenly felt fingers run lightly up his back and he turned sharply.

A girl wearing a veil and nothing else—her body glistening with oil—smiled seductively and reached up to pull his head down. In one motion Cord grabbed her at the waist and heaved her at what appeared to be a pile of animal skins. He strode off angrily, then glanced back to make certain the girl was not injured.

She was neither injured, nor showing any disappointment over the rejection. The pile of animal skins apparently had taut canvas under them, and she was bouncing high in the air, laughing and spreading her legs with each bounce. As Cord watched, a nude tumbler jumped on the skins and bounced with her. Then they were suddenly joined, and the girl squealed with delight as they bounced higher and higher.

Cord walked on. Ahead of him, the big Turk who had been massaging the bull was filling a goatskin from a tilted barrel. When Cord approached, the man smiled and lifted the goatskin, motioning for Cord to drink.

Cord opened his mouth and the liquid that streamed over his lips and tongue had the acrid taste of fermented grapes.

The man smiled again, handed Cord the goatskin, and strode off. Cord spat out the liquid as quickly as the man was gone. Aside from his vows against drinking alcoholic spirits, he had no intention of becoming a part of this mob of madmen. He hung the goatskin on a hook and looked around.

Could this place possibly be considered a rose in the wilderness? To Cord, it was more accurately a cesspool. The bull the Turk had been massaging was now being carried to a huge open-pit fire. The animal had been halved and spitted, and four men hoisted the two pieces in place over the flames. A crowd of people shouted and clapped as the fire danced and leaped around the sizzling flesh.

A greater noise came from behind Cord, and he quickly turned. Five Bedouin horsemen came galloping past the tents and wheeled into the clearing. The horses reared and snorted, and the riders fired their rifles into the air. Then the horsemen turned and galloped off to another clearing.

Cord edged back between two tents. He suddenly felt confused and overwhelmed by the frenzy of noise and activity. The madness surrounding him made no sense. Why were these people camped in the middle of the desert? Unless he was given some indication that there was a trial here, he saw no reason to remain.

He breathed deeply and rhythmically and closed his eyes, calming his thoughts. He could gather enough food, and a goatskin of water, and easily make it across the desert now. This encampment had no purpose for him. It was a group of traveling entertainers—a corrupt collection of degenerates who chanced to be crossing the desert at the same time he was. They had no interest in him, and they had no connection with Zetan and the trials.

Cord sensed a strange presence as his mind finally settled. He opened his eyes enough to make out blurred forms, and then he blinked, focusing on the pink figure gazing silently at him from ten paces away.

It was a woman—a girl, more accurately. In her pink kaftan, and her face covered in purdah, Cord could see only her darkened eyes. The pupils were dark brown pools, liquid and smouldering. As she stared at him her gaze was both questioning and knowing.

Cord smiled, and a faint shadow seemed to cross the girl's face. He stepped forward. "Can you tell me . . . ?" As quickly as he spoke, the girl turned sharply and hurried away.

Cord tried to follow her. He stepped out from between the tents and pushed his way through the crowd of moving people. But she was gone, swallowed up by the flowing tangle of bodies. Trying to glimpse her somewhere ahead, he moved along with the traffic for a minute, but then he stopped. She was nowhere to be seen.

He watched as three naked dwarfs playing harmonicas marched by; then he stepped to the side as a huge black man wearing a red loincloth pushed his way through the crowd.

The man was at least a foot taller than Cord, and his bulging muscles glistening in the torchlight. Cord watched as people hastily stepped out of the giant's path. Then he followed along, almost running to keep up.

From the respectful way people looked at the man, he was either an important figure in the camp, or he could lead Cord to someone who was.

The giant finally made a sharp turn and disappeared into the velvet tent Cord had passed earlier. Cord followed him as far as the opening and then stopped at the side.

The cushions and low couches were now all occupied. Servants were moving through the crowd, delivering food and drinks on gold serving trays, and the clatter of voices and laughter was deafening.

Farther inside, at the center of the tent, the Turk with the long hair was seated on a dais between two unoccupied cushions. Cord watched as the big black man made his way through the crowd and sat down at the Turk's left. The two men smiled at each other, apparently friends, and a servant immediately placed a platter of food in front of the giant.

Cord glanced around at the other people and back to the Turk. Then he blinked uncertainly. The Turk was smiling directly at him, beckoning Cord to come in.

Cord stepped inside and circled the crowd, finally making his way to the dais. The Turk waved him to the unoccupied cushion on his right, and as he sat down Cord turned to speak to the man. But the Turk had turned away, talking to somebody far to his left. Then a servant leaned between them and spread food and wine in front of Cord.

Cord gazed at the platter of beef and steaming rice, then shook his head as the waiter offered gravy. A tureen of soup appeared; then silver bowls of strawberries and raisins and nuts.

The Turk was still talking—in a tongue Cord didn't understand. Cord noticed that the black man on the other cushion had pushed his food away and was sitting with his arms folded over his chest.

A strong scent of perfume suddenly filled the air, and Cord looked over his shoulder. Six robed girls were coming through a curtain and moving into positions behind the dais. Then six more appeared. Cord watched as they picked their way through, stepping over prone bodies. Then he looked up sharply as he saw the hem of a pink kaftan beneath one of the robes.

It was the same girl. Her eyes seemed to burn out at him from above her silken veil. Cord smiled, but there was no change in her expression.

Then it registered. The girl's kaftan was not pink —it was *rose*-colored! And it was the only rose kaftan in the group. Cord stared hard as the girl lowered herself onto a pillow. She returned the stare, but her smouldering eyes told him nothing.

He finally turned back, sensing that the Turk was watching him. The man's faint smile turned into a broad grin.

102

"Have you eaten? Where is your drink? Your hand is empty."

Cord returned the man's smile. "Peace."

"Peace?!" The man's voice roared over the clamor of noise. "Don't wash it on *me!*" He laughed and made a sweeping gesture. "The whole world is in commotion, and you wish me peace! Hah! I don't know what peace is! I don't want it! Haven't you listened to the desert? Even when there is no wind the sand sings. Girls walk by and there's the silken sound of their thighs. Why, that alone's enough to burst a man's eardrums."

Cord nodded, uncertain how to respond. "My name is Cord," he said.

The Turk laughed again. "You see? Cord! Play a chord, strike a chord! Even your name is a noise! What do you want, Cord? Do you want us to play on you?" He grinned and leaned closer. "My wife can make your skin sing. She'll play a few pretty tunes on your belly. What do you say?"

"Who are you?" Cord asked.

"Changsha!" the man answered proudly. "And what is it you want? It is my wish to provide what is needed. What is it you need so that I can find happiness by providing it for you?"

Cord glanced across at the girl. "I seek a rose in the wilderness," he said.

"Her name is Tara," Changsha said, "My ninth wife."

Cord frowned, but the man did not seem to be offended. "Forgive me. I did not know."

Changsha shrugged. "You may have her."

"You honor me. But I have taken a vow of chastity."

"Taking her will be a double sacrifice—for her, of her vows to me—for you, of your vows to yourself."

Cord leaned close to the man. "Look at me," he said. "Look closely at me."

Changsha looked Cord up and down. "Your nose is burnt from the sun. Your eyes are faded from the sun. You smell of the sun. So?"

"I am looking for Zetan," Cord said.

"Ahhh! The Keeper of the Book! Yes, I know of Zetan. He can strike so quickly he can break silk!"

"You have seen him do this?"

The man's eyes narrowed, and he considered the question. "It is *said* that he can do this."

"My Second Trial?" Cord asked. "Is it with you?"

"Perhaps." The man gave him an innocent smile. "Who knows? Do you know?"

"Is this . . . ?" Cord gestured around the crowd. "Is this all yours?"

"In so far as anything *belongs* to a man, it is all mine." The Turk suddenly dropped his eyes and frowned as if some dark thought crossed his mind. He turned sharply and stared at the black giant on his left.

The man still had not touched his food. With Changsha staring at him now, he took a red candle and ceremoniously lighted it. Then he rose, and with the candle held at arm's length, he strode from the dais.

A hush fell over the crowd, and everybody watched the black giant stride out. Then, as if on signal, everyone except Changsha and his wives quickly rose and headed for the door. Cord watched as the crowd surged out of the tent, apparently excited about something.

When he turned back to Changsha, the Turk was gone. Behind him, Changsha's wives were also gone. Cord frowned, watching the last of the crowd leave through the door. For some reason the giant's striding out of the tent with a lighted candle had emptied the place. He finally decided to follow.

The crowd outside was so large, he could see nothing. He moved to the side and stepped up on a barrel.

A huge Persian rug was spread on the sand, and torches were burning at each of the corners. On the far side, a mixed group of musicians was gathering. Next to them were jugglers, tumblers, concubines, naked slave girls, warriors, robed and veiled women, all quietly taking what appeared to be assigned positions.

On the carpet, the black giant was now wearing a red sash around his head. He was going through a martial arts *kata:* striking out at an imaginary enemy, then drawing back, then whirling to face another unseen attacker. The crowd watched in respectful silence.

On the left, the people suddenly opened a path, and Changsha's wives filed through. They stepped up to a raised platform and positioned themselves behind an elaborately carved throne-chair.

Tara, the girl in the rose kaftan, was third from the left. As Cord stared at her, her eyes lifted and returned the gaze.

Cord had no idea what was going on. It appeared as if a martial arts contest was about to take place. But he couldn't understand the grave manner of the crowd.

Nor was he certain what to make of the girl in the rose kaftan. Cord was certain she was the rose in the wilderness Jungar had told him to look for. But now that he had found her, did it mean he was to fight Changsha? Or by crossing the desert had he already passed his Second Trial?

Cord's thoughts were interrupted by a piercing cry from the left. There was movement in the shadows, and from above the spectators a body suddenly came hurtling through the air. An instant later, Changsha landed on the rug opposite the black giant.

He too had a red sash around his head, and he was holding a lighted candle exactly like the one the black man had carried from the tent. He lifted the candle toward the giant, and one of the warriors stepped forward and took it from his hand. The warrior moved to the corner and placed it in a holder next to the giant's candle.

Changsha gazed silently at the giant, then nodded. "This is your need? To test yourself against me?"

The giant was now standing as if at attention, his face solemn. "It is my need," he said with a powerful voice.

Changsha smiled. "Then come, my black friend. Put out your hand for what you feel will satisfy you."

Changsha appeared relaxed and confident, and the slight smile remained on his face as the giant stepped forward and assumed a fighting stance. The thumping of a drum suddenly broke the silence—a slow, deliberate, heartbeat rhythm. The

106

giant stiffened, then took a deep breath and once more assumed his stance.

Changsha appeared to be amused by his opponent's efforts to concentrate. He swayed slightly to the left and then the right, his movements fluid and rhythmical. Then, with no warning, he seemed to explode in a screaming lightning-fast attack.

The giant jumped back, retaliating with a barrage of expertly timed kicks and punches. Neither of the men landed a significant blow, and Changsha seemed to float away from the giant. He appeared to be dancing, his arms and shoulders swaying to the rhythm of the drumbeats. He moved from side to side, and then circled, staying only a fraction of an inch beyond the reach of the giant.

The big black man finally stepped out of range, clearly dissatisfied with the manner in which the battle had begun. He took another breath and moved into his stance again, once more trying to concentrate.

Changsha instantly faked an attack, first low, then high, and the giant tried to counter with blocks, combined with attacks of his own. Again he failed to score, and again he was pursuing Changsha and falling into the Turk's rhythm. The giant drove forward with a knife-hand thrust and then a roundhouse kick.

Both missed, and as if by signal, the drumbeats suddenly stopped. At the same instant, Changsha darted in with a front kick, a forefist to the giant's chin, and then a side kick to the shoulder that staggered the giant. The big man dropped a hand to the carpet and stopped himself from falling. Then he reassumed his stance and came cautiously forward. The drumbeat started once again, and once again Changsha moved with the rhythm, watching dispassionately as he weaved sinuously in and out.

It was clear to Cord that Changsha was fighting a psychological battle, and the drumming and sudden silences were all a part of it. The steady thumping seemed to unnerve the giant, and the silences were a signal that Changsha was going to attack. But instead of preparing the giant, they were an additional strain on his concentration.

Three times the sequence was repeated. The drum beats continued until the giant reached a point of frustration and failed in a desperate attack. Then they stopped while Changsha delivered a combination of punishing blows. When Changsha finished his attack and resumed the rhythmical dance, the drum once again resumed its maddening beat.

The giant was now soaked with perspiration. With his jaw clenched tight and his eyes narrowed with concentration, he came forward again. It was clear that the man was desperate and no longer in complete control of himself. Changsha, on the other hand, looked almost bored. He knew his opponent was beaten. And while the drum continued to thump, he weaved in and out offering the giant tempting targets.

The black man finally exploded. With an angry roar he stepped forward and leaped high in the air to deliver a desperate roundhouse kick. Changsha's head was directly in front of the driving foot, and then it was half an inch below it. When the man landed, Changsha was within inches of him. With the drum suddenly silenced again, he delivered a quick inverted fist to the man's chin and then drove both fists into the abdomen. There was a twisting movement in the blows and the giant seemed to quiver for an instant as he opened his mouth in a silent scream. Then, with a dying gasp in his throat, he doubled forward and dropped heavily to the rug.

It was over. The black man's body quivered with quick spasms for a minute. Then the breathing stopped, and the eyes turned dull.

Changsha gazed silently at the body, as if making certain the man was dead. Then he turned and walked to the two burning candles. He threw a punch at the giant's candle, and the buffeted air snuffed out the challenger's flame.

Cord grimaced as he stared at the giant's inert form sprawled across the rug. Jungar, the monkey-man, had been a vicious fighter. But even he had not taken the lives of his mangled victims.

Six of Changsha's warriors rolled the black body over. They folded the man's arms over his chest and then carried him to a high platform off to the side. The drums began a ceremonious beat, and then bells and cymbals joined in.

The crowd watched in respectful silence as one of the warriors touched a flaming torch to the tightly stacked pyre of kindling under the platform. Changsha then motioned the warriors back. He moved in dangerously close to the flames, his head lifted as though watching the man's spirit rise into the night.

The drums and bells and cymbals continued their funereal beat until the flames enveloped the body. Then the entire platform was a raging inferno.

The man was being burned as a hero. He was being given a tribute for his courage and his sacrifice. Cord jumped down from the barrel and moved through the crowd, almost to the funeral pyre.

Changsha was still gazing upward. "You came to me to test yourself," he said solemnly. "And in losing, you gained your victory. For now you are on the threshold of truth. You know now that when you were alive you were dead, and only thought yourself alive. That knowledge, that gift —which is what you really wanted from me—you have it now."

Changsha turned and looked at the crowd. When he spotted Cord he smiled.

"When do we fight?" Cord asked.

"After we *sleep,* my boy," the Turk said and strode off.

Cord watched the man disappear into the big tent. Then the crowd began dispersing. The festivities seemed to be over for the day. The musicians, the jugglers, the naked women; all were trudging off to their tents. Cord was alone again.

He turned back to the funeral pyre. The flames had now consumed the platform. With a shower of sparks, the platform suddenly collapsed.

So this would be his Second Trial, Cord reflected. He would either end up in a heap of smouldering charcoal, or he would set out across the desert again with Changsha in his bowl. The first Trial was a monkey-man, and now Changsha, the rhythm-man. But in this case, Ah Sahm was not around to give him a demonstration of how to beat his opponent.

A few campfires were still smouldering, but

110

there wasn't a soul in sight as Cord walked slowly among the tents. It was very inhospitable of Changsha, Cord thought, not to provide a place to sleep. Then he stopped and gazed off through the darkness.

A small, rather shabby-looking tent was standing by itself at the edge of a clearing. The canvas door was thrown back, and it appeared to be unoccupied. Cord moved closer and looked in.

There were a dozen or so pillows strewn around a rug. In the center was a small bowl with a flickering candle. Cord moved inside and pulled the flap down behind him. He glanced into the second room—a bathing room that was also unoccupied. Then he brought several pillows close to the candle and sat down in a lotus position. He closed his eyes and breathed deeply, letting his thoughts settle slowly in his mind.

Was it possible this was the final trial, he wondered. Could the Turk also be Zetan? And did he live in this manner because the Book had shown him this was the truth and the path to wisdom? The possibility was staggering to Cord. All his life he had been taught that hedonism was the greatest enemy of wisdom. Was it possible that his teachers had been mistaken? The idea was too startling to contemplate.

He pushed the thought from his mind and once more breathed deeply, settling his thoughts.

"It is like a churning, muddy lake filled with flotsam and jetsam," Lo Tzu told him when speaking of the mind. "The incoming rivers must be cut off and we must hold it perfectly still. In time, the debris will drift to the bottom and the mud will slowly settle. Ultimately the water will be

111

clear. and we will see all things with perfect clarity."

Cord held his mind still. He felt his neck and shoulder muscles relax, and he envisioned flotsam and jetsam drifting quietly to the bottom of his mind. The muddiness was gradually thinning, and there was a faint light filtering through.

VII

Cord was too deeply immersed in his meditation to hear any external sounds. There was the faint patter of bare feet on the sand in front of the tent. Then the flap was drawn aside a few inches, and the girl slipped through with her tray of food. She placed the tray on a pillow in front of Cord, and then brought more pillows from the corners of the tent. On the tray were several steaming dishes in crockery pots, and a long-stemmed rose.

The girl dropped to her knees beside Cord and very gently opened his shirt. Then she drew it over his shoulders and down his arms. He stirred slightly, but his arms were limp and his eyes remained closed. She set the shirt aside and gazed curiously at him, waiting.

The perfume filtered slowly into Cord's senses. Then he became aware of food smells and the faint sound of breathing. His eyelids flickered and lifted a fraction. Then he stopped breathing and stared.

The girl's veiled face was within inches of his, her dark, dilated eyes too close to focus on. He brought his hands to his bared chest and his absent shirt.

The girl was smiling. Cord glanced at the closed tent flap and at the tray of food. He was finally awake, and at least partially recovered from the initial shock. He frowned at the tray again, then reached out and touched the rose.

"It pleases you?" the girl asked.

Cord was not sure if it pleased him or not. He nodded and glanced suspiciously around the tent. "Where is . . . ?"

"No harm will come to you," she said. "My husband has sent me to you."

"Your husband . . ." Cord squinted closely at her in the flickering light. "Your husband . . . is he Zetan?"

She looked puzzled, then her voice was sweet and innocent. "My husband is Changsha."

"Not the Keeper of the Book?"

"What book?"

Cord was satisfied that if Changsha had another identity, the girl was unaware of it. Her eyes were too pure and innocent to disguise a falsehood.

She leaned forward and lifted the cover from a small silver pot. The fresh clean scent of her black hair prompted Cord to take a deep, steadying breath. Her graceful movements and the rustling of silk were almost too tantalizing for him to bear.

114

"Why did he send you?" Cord asked. "I told him I've taken a vow of . . ."

The girl smiled and sat back. "This will not violate your vow. The desired fruit may be enjoyed without consumption. Just as one enjoys the breath of God without having to die."

Cord frowned at her, not sure he understood. Then he suddenly laughed, remembering the man in the barrel. "Like a knife," he said.

She blinked at him, puzzled. "A knife?"

"Like a sword!" Cord said. He lifted the silver por and looked closely at the liquid inside. "The oil!" He laughed and held the pot in front of him. "If this pot were bigger, I could jump into it!" He laughed again, the ludicrous image of the man in the barrel once again coming to him.

The girl was frowning more deeply, as if uncertain about his sanity.

"No, no, please," Cord assured her, "I'm all right. Don't be afraid. It's just . . ."

She brought her hand up and placed a finger on his lips as if to calm him. This movement caused her uncinched breasts to sway tantalizingly through her robe. Cord closed his eyes and took a long, steadying breath. "I've been traveling a long time," he said.

Her fingers traced the outline of his mouth and brushed across his cheek. "Rest," she said quietly. "You are tired."

Cord kept his eyes closed. He could shut out the sight of her, but the perfume and the sound of her movements remained. "I've been taking a journey that was indicated in my palm," he said.

He felt her fingers touch his hand. She stroked it gently, then lifted it to her mouth. The soft lips kissed the center of his palm, then moved slowly around the edges.

Cord knew he must try to stop her. But the warmth and tenderness seemed to ease all the aches and pains of his traveling. Her lips were incredibly soft, and a shudder went through his body with each new spot she kissed.

"Did you know," he asked, "that you could walk the line in your hand for a lifetime?" He opened his eyes and quickly lifted her face from his hand. "Stop. Please. Stop. Look at me!"

She lifted her eyes and gazed questioningly at him. Her face was beautiful—a face that Cord had seen many times in his dreams. Until now he had never believed such beauty existed.

"You are my trial, aren't you?" he challenged.

She frowned again, searching his eyes.

"Answer me!" Cord demanded.

"Let me walk the line of your palm with you for a moment," she said softly.

"No, I . . ."

Her eyes were gently pleading and her lips were parted. Cord gazed back at her for a minute. Then he grabbed her arms and pulled her close, holding her fiercely. Just as abruptly he thrust her back and turned away.

He was a fool to let her stay in the tent with him. Or was he a fool to reject her? Desire surged in his loins, and his vow of chastity seemed to grow more dim and distant. It had been a promise made in a void.

"Let me show you," the girl said softly.

Cord heard the rustle of movement. He took a deep breath and looked at her again.

She was standing now, smiling gently at him

116

as her hands parted the robe and let it drop to the carpet.

Cord caught his breath. Her body was as beautiful as her face—full, ripe, sensual, but still fresh with youth. He looked at the gently composed face, the deliciously firm breasts, the narrow waist and smooth belly, and he closed his eyes.

The vow was now lost in the clamoring of his desires. Cord came slowly to his feet and stood perfectly still as the girl removed the last of his garments. She touched her lips to his neck and his breastbone, then took him by the hand and led him quietly through the door to the second room.

The pink marble bath was filled with water and lightly steaming. She stepped in and smiled, holding a hand out for him. Cord eased himself into the warm water.

His heart thudded heavily against his ribs, and with his head resting back, his gaze devoured the beautiful mouth, the slender neck and shoulders, and the smooth contour of the breasts as they floated at the level of the water. The nipples were dark and full and succulent.

She moved toward him with a small sponge and Cord drew her close, kissing her roughly on the mouth. Then he drew her body upward and took a nipple in his lips.

"No," she said gently, her voice barely audible. She brought her face close to his and kissed his eyes and nose and cracked lips. "Not yet," she said. "It is forbidden during the bath."

Cord released her, and her lips moved slowly down his neck and chest and then to his stomach before she drew back. Then she smiled and quietly bathed herself.

Cord lay back and watched, half intoxicated by the sinuous, caressing movements. It was as if she were carefully preparing each part of her body for him, at the same time smiling with anticipation over the pleasure it was going to bring.

Finally she stepped out. Her movements were graceful and delicate, and Cord could see that her heart was also beating heavily.

She dried herself with a scented towel. When she was done, Cord stepped out and she did the same for him, gently stroking the towel over every part of his body, lightly kissing the skin after it was dry. Then she lifted a decanter and let drops of perfume fall on her neck and shoulders. With her fingertips, she lightly brushed the drops over her breasts and down her abdomen. She did the same to Cord, lightly massaging his chest and stomach. She finally closed her eyes and drew Cord's mouth to her scented breasts. Then she led him back to the other room and to the bed of pillows.

Later, Cord was never able to remember the sequence of their lovemaking. It was sweet and it was violent, and at times they were quiet and motionless. At other times, he doubted the reality of his previous existence. Tara was now the only truth he would ever know, or would ever want to know. Her passion was the only food he needed. She was part of him, and he was part of her, and they were coupled forever.

They slept, and when they awakened they once again affirmed their need for each other. Cord held her tight, and for a long time she clasped his head to her breast. When Cord finally moved to kiss her, there were tears in her eyes.

Cord frowned and lightly brushed the tears away, then kissed the eyes. "Tara? Why are you crying?"

"I must go," she said hesitantly.

"Why?"

"I have to go back to Changsha."

Cord stared at her, not believing her words. She couldn't possible be serious. "You're *never* going back to him," he said emphatically.

Her eyes suddenly darkened with fear and confusion. "What do you mean?"

"You're going with me!"

Cord had not considered the words until he spoke them. But he knew they were true. He loved the girl, and he would not leave without her.

She shook her head, her eyes wide. "But where? How can I . . . ?"

Cord took her hand and held it tightly. "You can't say no, Tara. You love me. Tell me!"

"Yes, I do, but . . . but my place is here. And you are looking for Zetan."

"We'll go together. We'll find him together."

"No, please . . ." She shook her head and looked away.

"I want you!"

She touched her forehead as if unable to comprehend the situation. "But . . . this was to be . . . one night . . . only one. . . ."

Cord felt his heart sink, his anger at Changsha suddenly flaring. The man had no right to treat the girl like a slave. Cord grabbed her arms and held them firmly. "No!" he said. "Changsha gives you away like a ring for a finger . . . a drink from a bottle. But I will not! You're mine now!"

119

She gazed back at him, confused, hurt—like a wounded animal. Tears suddenly burst from her eyes, and she threw her arms around his neck and held tightly. "Yes!" she said, "I love you! Take me with you!"

Cord closed his eyes and clung to her, rocking gently back and forth. She was not an apparition. Nor was she a slave to Changsha's commands. She was his, and he was hers. He kissed her ears and her cheeks and her eyes, and then held her in a long embrace.

"We must go," he finally said. "Quickly."

Except for the sounds of sleeping and the occasional snort of an animal, the encampment was silent. Cord stood outside the tent, listening. Tara joined him, once more dressed in her robes.

As they moved past the litter-strewn clearings, Cord picked up some apples and pears and dropped them in his pouch. At the perimeter of the camp he paused, cautioning Tara to silence.

The only sentry he could see was sitting cross-legged in the sand, his head drooped forward. They moved quietly past and up the high mound of sand dunes. When they reached the top, Cord looked back. There was still no movement in the camp.

A slight breeze was blowing, and Cord set out at a fast pace toward the eastern horizon. Her hand firmly grasped in his, Tara alternately walked and ran to keep up. If necessary, he would carry her, Cord decided.

Once they were out of sight of the camp, Cord smiled ruefully, thinking about the events of the last twelve hours. Was it possible he had now passed the Second Trial? Instead of its being a test of his strength and courage and skill in the martial arts, was it a test of his love and compassion and loyalty? If he had demonstrated his love for Tara and then abandoned her, perhaps Changsha would then have informed him that he had failed.

Why not? he asked himself. Were not those virtues as important as conquering enemies in battle? And would not a man be judged a coward if he took his pleasures with a woman and then left her in the bondage of a mad Turk? Cord glanced back at Tara and felt pleased with himself. He had rescued her not for selfish reasons, but at what seemed great risk to his mission. He had acted honorably and correctly, he decided. In all probability he had now passed the Second Trial.

An hour later they had left the desert behind, and they climbed into a rocky canyon. A small stream trickled down from somewhere above, and they finally came upon a deep pond within a small grove of trees. They both drank greedily, and then Cord cleared an area for them on the sandy bank.

"We will continue traveling in the morning?" Tara asked when they lay down.

"Yes," Cord answered. He kissed her gently and smoothed her hair away from her face.

"Where will you go to find Zetan?"

Cord did not know for sure. Beyond finding a rose in the wilderness, he had no further instructions. "We will be shown the way," he said. "Don't worry."

121

"I am not worried."

"Sleep," Cord said. "It will be dawn in a few hours."

She embraced him tightly and then was asleep.

Cord kissed her lightly on the forehead and eased out of her arms. With his hands behind his head, he gazed thoughtfully at the stars.

He thought about Changsha and Jungar, and then wondered idly how the monkey-man had known about the rose in the desert. Clearly it was all prearranged in some way. But if Morthond had beaten Jungar, would he too have been directed to the rose? And would he have fallen in love with her?

Cord doubted it. Morthond had been a dedicated man with his thoughts dominated by a single idea. And it was precisely that single-mindedness that had led to his downfall. Morthond was like the saber-toothed tiger. The animal had been so intent on becoming an efficient killer, the muscles holding its huge teeth grew larger and more powerful until they cramped its brain into stupidity and extinction. With Morthond, his narrow vision had been limited to the perfection of a single fighting style. And like the green-robed man Cord had watched fight Jungar, he had been unable to cope with the unorthodox ways of the monkey-man.

Cord closed his eyes and wondered if his desire to find Zetan and the Book of Wisdom was still as compelling as before. If a man was happy, did he need as much wisdom? And for his happiness, did he need anything more than Tara?

He opened his eyes as a brief gust of wind buffeted across the canyon and sent pebbles trickling down from the rocks above. Then there was silence again. It was as if a storm was making tentative probes at the mountain.

Unaccountably, Cord felt an odd shiver go down his spine. It was weariness, he decided. He listened for another minute and then closed his eyes to sleep.

Cord was dimly conscious of an insect buzzing around his face. He lifted a hand and brushed it away. He took a deep, satisfying breath and suddenly felt the searing warmth of the sun on his face. Once again he brushed at the insect. Then he opened his eyes and squinted at the dazzling white sky.

The sun was coming over the rocky walls of the canyon. It was almost noon! Cord smiled ruefully at his own laziness, then rose on an elbow and turned to Tara.

The impression from her body was still visible in the soft sand. But she was no longer there. He glanced around the pond, then looked behind him.

Had she gone off in search of food? Or maybe farther up the canyon? Cord came quickly to his feet and peered up the narrowing corridor of rock. "Tara!"

He listened, hearing only the quiet trickle of water and the buzzing of insects. He quickly climbed to the top of a huge rock where he could see the canyon fanning out in the desert below. "T-a-a-a-r-a," he shouted.

His heart thudded heavily in his chest as he heard his voice slowly fade away into silence. Light gusts of intermittent wind were sweeping across the desert, and there was no answer from

123

below. He moved toward the pool again and looked around the sandy bank. He saw no slippers, or scarves, or any indications of her having been there. Nor were any footprints discernible in the rocky canyon bottom.

Cord grabbed up his pouch and started down the canyon, walking at first, then running. "Tara!" he called out and glanced at the canyon walls.

When he reached the sand dunes there were no footprints. Even those they had made the night before had been swept over by the wind. He ran, stumbling over the dunes, racing back in the direction of Changsha's camp.

He could see no flags, nor the tops of any tents rising over the high mound of dunes. He staggered up the hill, falling, scrambling to his feet, his heart pounding with fear as he finally reached the top. Then he gasped, not breathing for a minute as he stared at the empty, desolate stretch of sand below. Changsha and his caravan were gone.

He lifted his eyes, scanning the far horizon and the hills to the east. Then he turned back sharply, sensing something odd in the empty campsite. Rising from the hollow at the base of the hill there appeared to be the uppermost tips of three long poles. The broad, plateau-like top of the hill blocked his view of anything below.

Cord moved forward; slowly at first, then gathering speed as he saw more and more of the poles. Then his mouth came open in an agonized, silent scream, and he staggered on. "T-a-a-a-r-a!" he cried.

The tripod of heavy poles met ten feet in the air and the three ends extended upward another ten feet. Just above the crossing point, Tara's wrists were bound to two of the poles, her outspread legs straddling the apex. Her head was hanging limply to the side, her lifeless eyes staring down at the empty sand below.

"Tara!" Cord cried out hoarsely as he reached the tripod and gazed up at her. Her mouth was partially open, but the beautiful face was expressionless. Her skin was discolored in spots, already hardening in the desert heat. What had once provided love and warmth and tenderness was now a corpse.

A gust of wind lifted a lock of hair and fluttered it for a moment. Then it dropped limply to her breast. Cord stared, then felt his heart plunge even deeper. At the side of her head, hanging crookedly from her ear, was a withered rose.

Cord gazed at her for a long time. Then he closed his eyes and rested his forehead against one of the poles. He was trembling, and his breath came in shaky gasps.

He finally looked up again. Tara was still gazing emptily at the ground. Cord felt anger slowly rising within him, slowly consuming the pain and agony. "Changsha," he said with quiet bitterness.

He looked at the empty campsite and then the desert beyond. "Changsha!" he screamed.

He turned from the poles and loped into the center of the clearing where Changsha's tent had been. "Changsha!" he cried out, and turned sharply around as if expecting the big Turk to materialize behind him. "Changsha!" he cried again. Then he ran.

He was not conscious of the direction he was

going. He didn't care. He ran faster and faster, screaming at the wind and the desert and the distant mountains. The angry tears streamed down his cheeks as he stumbled across the dunes, screaming louder and louder.

VIII

Cord trudged onward through the rocky, desert-like hills. The brush tore at his legs, and the rocks and sand scraped and burned the soles of his feet. But he kept moving, his eyes set on no particular destination.

Occasionally he stopped. He sat on a rock and his head sagged between his knees as he stared vacantly at the sand beneath him. At one stop, a scorpion as large as his hand moved across in front of him. The shiny orange-brown creature came at him in fits and starts, its deadly tail curved above its flanks as if anxiously searching for a victim. It moved to within an inch of Cord's toe where it pondered the situation for a full minute before it moved on.

A vulture followed him for several miles. The grotesque bird made broad circles above him, soaring effortlessly in front and then behind—as if calculating just how much longer Cord would last in the broiling heat, and if it was worthwhile hanging around. Finally it circled to a higher altitude and drifted silently off to the south.

At mid-afternoon Cord perched himself on a low promontory and forced himself to meditate. But he could not drive the image of Tara spread-eagled on the poles from his mind. For ten minutes he droned through a mantra, trying to imagine his mind a total void. Then he breathed deeply and let his body sag. At last some peace came. He thought about Lo Tzu and the other monks at the monastery, and of the peaceful gardens with their flowing fountains.

He heard a flute, with its low-register notes that seemed to vibrate the earth and rocks. The notes rose higher, forming more mellow tones, followed by an eerie dance of half-tones that was both strident and soothing.

He finally opened his eyes, and for the first time in hours, looked at his surroundings. To the east and west the desert continued as far as the eye could see. To the north, the mountains rose sharply into formidable snow-covered peaks.

To the south there were also mountains. But their slopes were green, and there appeared to be a pass angling through them. Cord slid down from the rocky promontory and headed south across the desert. His stride was now firmer, more resolute. There was no more reason to go through the mountain pass than there was to continue on through the desert or to scale the higher mountains. But for some reason he felt drawn to the south. The desert now seemed a wasteland of evil and corruption.

A short distance out of the desert there were patches of green. Gnarled poplar trees lined the banks of a dry riverbed, and scattered clumps of bunch-grass covered the banks. Cord followed the sandy course of the river for several miles before the first stagnant pools began to appear. Finally the growth became greener and more lush, and tall trees grew along the sides of a trickling brook.

The brook led him to a larger stream, which came rushing down from what appeared to be a broad valley higher in the mountains. From somewhere ahead, he could hear the hiss and roar of a waterfall. Cord quickened his pace as he followed the path up the canyon. He finally saw it: a thundering rush of water cascading into a rocky gorge.

The pool beneath the falls was broad and clear and surrounded by trees. When he reached the shore, Cord dropped his pouch and made his way around to the slippery ledge below the falls. He stepped under the roaring cascade and let it batter his head and shoulders.

The water was cold and clean, and the driving weight seemed to cleanse his mind and pound all feeling from his flesh. He dropped his head from one side to the other and lifted his arms, luxuriating in the coolness. His skin tingled and his mouth and nose and throat were clean, and he **was no longer encased in dust and grit and** stinging sand.

He finally sat down on the ledge, and with the

water still pounding his knees and legs, he leaned his head back and closed his eyes. The thunderous roar of the water plunging into the pool inundated his whole being, and he surrendered gratefully to it.

After several minutes a voice seemed to drift through the roar. It was distant and light, but the words were clear and echoed faintly. "You cannot do it," the voice said. "You cannot do it."

Cord opened his eyes and listened, certain he must be hearing things. Once again the words filtered through the roar. He propped himself up and squinted through the crashing wall of water.

A shadowy form was moving slowly toward him from the lower end of the pool. Cord slid from the ledge and ducked past the waterfall and into the deep water. When he surfaced he eased to where his feet could touch bottom.

The figure coming toward him was Ah Sahm. He was walking in the middle of the stream, head down moving very slowly, taking one step at a time.

"You cannot do it," Ah Sahn said as if talking to himself. "You cannot do it."

Cord watched until the man was several yards into the pool. Then Ah Sahm stopped and lifted his head as if fully aware of Cord's gaze.

"You can't do *what?*" Cord shouted against the thunder of the cascading water.

Ah Sahm frowned and lowered his head again. He took another tentative step. "You cannot step twice on the same piece of water."

Cord laughed, glad to see the old man again. He swam a few strokes and then walked to the shore where he had left his pouch. "Why would you want to step on the same piece of water twice?"

Ah Sahm came slowly out of the pool. He passed Cord and climbed up the slope to the rocky area above the waterfall. "Wanting has nothing to do with it," he said.

Cord picked up his pouch and followed. Above the falls, the stream tumbled and thrashed over boulders and moss-covered rocks. After he had walked along the bank for some distance, Ah Sahm moved to the water's edge and once again stepped in. The current was slower now, and using the rocks as stepping stones, he carefully made his way upstream.

Several times he stopped and seemed to listen to the warbling and chattering of birds in the surrounding trees. He seemed to have no destination in mind, no goal aside from enjoying what he found in his surroundings. Cord moved along the bank, watching him.

Ahead of them, in a thick growth of trees, a small waterfall emptied into a quiet pool. Ah Sahm seemed to sense the peaceful beauty of the spot. When he reached it, he waded into the pool and stood so quietly that Cord began to wonder if the man was still breathing. Then Ah Sahm's hand eased quietly into the water and once again he was like a statue. When the hand finally came up, a fish was wriggling in its fingers. Ah Sahm waded across and stepped up on a broad, flat rock.

"A fish saved my life once," he said.

"How?"

"I ate him."

Cord smiled, but the man's face remained

131

expressionless. Ah Sahm was standing on the rock now, the fish still wriggling in his hand.

"Give me your knife" Ah Sahm said, reaching out.

Cord moved to the rock and handed over the knife.

The old man sat down and expertly cleaned and skinned the fish. He sliced it down the middle and handed back Cord's knife. He gave half the raw fish to Cord, then pulled small chunks of flesh from the bones and put them methodically into his mouth.

Cord also ate. The fish was tender and had a delicate taste. "How did you get across the desert?" he asked.

The man's sightless eyes were gazing across the pond as if studying the trees on the other side. He continued to put pieces of fish in his mouth, but he said nothing.

The stream apparently came from a valley six or eight miles ahead and several thousand feet above them. On either side, the mountains rose sharply into rocky peaks. Cord wondered if the man was headed for the high valley. If so, where did he intend to go after he passed through the valley?

"Why do you do that?" Ah Sahm suddenly asked.

Cord stared, not sure what the man was talking about. "Do what?"

"Chew twenty-one times on the left side of your jaw, and then twenty-one times on the right, before you swallow?"

Cord was not aware that his chewing habits

were so precise or obvious. It was a routine he had developed many years ago, and he was hardly conscious of it any more. "I was taught that in the monastery."

"By a deaf monk, obviously," Ah Sahm said. "Does it serve a purpose?"

Cord thought for a minute, trying to remember all the reasons. "It exercises the jaw. It prepares the stomach to receive the food, and it extracts the essence of each mouthful."

Ah Sahm snorted, shaking his head. "A hungry man who was disciplined in that manner might starve to death while still counting."

Cord smiled, but the old man's face was still expressionless.

"It does one other thing, as well," Ah Sahm added.

"What is that?"

"It annoys powerfully. Were you unhealthy before you learned to eat in that manner?"

"No."

"Are you healthier now that you do?"

Cord considered the question, then shrugged. "No."

"But you nevertheless continue to follow the rules you were taught."

"It was part of my training! I listen to what I'm taught, and I obey my superiors."

Ah Sahm nodded. "Ahhh. You obey your superiors."

"I do."

"Then stop it."

Cord gaped at the man, then swallowed the lump of half-chewed fish that was still in his

133

mouth. He took smaller bites of the remaining fish, now finding himself overly conscious of his jaw movements.

Ah Sahm was finished. He lifted his head as though studying the higher mountains—or was he still counting Cord's jaw movements? Cord stuffed the last of the fish in his mouth and swallowed it after a few quick chews. Then he felt angry with himself for having complied so readily with the man's command.

Ah Sahm suddenly rose and moved away. He stepped off the rock and once more walked upstream, this time taking the path along the riverbank.

"Where are you going?" Cord called out.

There was no response. Cord hurriedly returned his knife to its sheath, picked up his pouch, and followed.

Ah Sahm was walking slowly, but he no longer seemed interested in the sounds of the water. The trail circled around boulders and at times was blocked by fallen trees. The man followed its course, stepping over the obstacles without hesitation.

"You still haven't told me your name," Cord said, following closely behind.

"You decided it was Ah Sahm. The thief."

"But you haven't told me your real name. Yet you saved my life."

"What I was not with you?"

"I mean your lesson with the monkey. It prepared me to face the First Trial."

"You saved your own life by listening."

Cord let out an exasperated sigh, wondering why he bothered asking the man questions. "If

134

you won't let me know your name," he said, "Tell me this: when did you go blind?"

"When did *you* go blind?" the man responded.

"I'm not blind."

"Am I?"

Cord stared at the man's back. "Do you answer every question with a question?"

"Do you question every answer?"

It was clearly hopeless. "You're like a wall I bounce myself off!" Cord said.

"Buddha sat down before a wall in the Deer Park at Benares," the man said after a silence. "When he arose, he was enlightened."

"You compare yourself with Buddha?"

"Only with the wall."

"You will drive me crazy!"

"Aren't you already crazy to talk to a wall?"

Cord groaned, clenching his fists for a moment. For once the man was quite right. He was indeed crazy to be talking to a man who was a wall.

Almost imperceptibly, Ah Sahm's pace had increased, and Cord now found himself hurrying to keep up. Ahead, Ah Sahm was gliding along with no apparent effort.

The trail turned away from the stream and passed through a thick forest of pines. When it emerged from the trees, they faced a rocky cliff that rose almost vertically for several hundred feet. A faint path no more than eight or ten inches wide angled up the side of the cliff and continued through a series of switchbacks. Ah Sahm didn't hesitate.

Cord stopped several times and looked down the precipitous drop below them. Then he found himself searching for handholds or roots, anything he could cling to. Ahead of him, Ah Sahm continued effortlessly upward, always perfectly balanced, never hesitating when he came to the turns or narrow ledges. He might have been a man out on an afternoon stroll.

The valley was not inhabited. The stream meandered slowly through grassy, pasture-like fields. In several places, Cord saw deer grazing. Ah Sahm strode through without a pause, and an hour later they climbed over a high pass and made their way down through a wooded slope.

The sea was now visible far to the left. Ah Sahm continued walking until the sun looked like a fiery red ball resting on the rim of the world. Ah Sahm then climbed to a high rock and settled himself in the lotus position. Cord did the same, and they silently watched the sun drop slowly into the sea.

Below them, and stretching off to the sea, were miles of valleys, mountain ranges, and richly cultivated flatlands. A hazy cloud was settling over the entire area, giving the terrain an eerie, surrealistic look.

"You have not mentioned your Second Trial," Ah Sahm said quietly. His sightless eyes were still fixed on the point where the sun had disappeared.

"It wasn't a trial," Cord answered softly. "It was a lesson."

"Teach it to me."

Cord smiled to himself. "You already know it. You seem to know everything."

Ah Sahm straightened and lifted his eyes a fraction. "Every morning when I awake . . . like a

136

scholar at his first class, I prepare a blank mind for the day to write on."

Cord gazed thoughtfully across the darkening valleys below. The night he had spent with Tara seemed like eons ago. And yet he could still smell the scent of her perfume. He could still feel her soft warm skin, and the silken texture of her hair. He could see her smile and hear her innocent, questioning voice.

"This lesson," Cord said, "was written on my heart. Only afterwards did my mind read it."

Ah Sahm turned his head away, as if to ease Cord's task.

"A year ago I took a vow of chastity," Cord said. "A day ago I broke it. I broke it gladly, because I realized that we are born to love."

He glanced at Ah Sahm, half expecting a comment. The old man was still motionless, scarcely breathing.

"But what I did was worse than taking any foolish vow," Cord said. "I tried to possess what I loved." He paused once more, looking over the hazy valleys. "The earth is made beautiful by the grass which grows on it," he said, "but the earth does not own the grass. Nor do the branches own their leaves. Nor the leaves the branches."

A great stillness seemed to envelop the land and sea below. The earth was spinning through its orbit and whirling around its poles, but not a leaf or pebble on its surface was stirring.

"Because I loved something, I thought I possessed it," Cord said quietly. "I didn't know that the embrace of love held too long will kill the loved one and the lover."

Darkness was now coming. The mountains and valleys stretching off to the sea were no more than vague shadows. Above the horizon Venus began to glimmer with a pale, questioning light.

"Cord," Ah Sahm said at length, "each moment that passes changes you. You do not—you cannot —even possess yourself. How could you possibly possess anyone or anything else?"

It was not a question to be answered: Cord had already affirmed the truth. Both men closed their eyes and breathed deeply, and the light of Venus pulsed and slowly grew more intense.

Cord was conscious of the darkness slowly draining from the sky. Somewhere nearby a small furry animal rustled across the rocks and then paused to look at them. It scampered away, sending bits of gravel trickling after it. Cord opened his eyes. Beside him, Ah Sahm appeared to be looking off at the sea. Slowly, Ah Sahm lifted his head, as if sensing the dawn behind him. Then he rose.

Cord did the same, and both men stood breathing deeply until the sun was half above the horizon. Without speaking, Ah Sahm turned and headed down the mountainside.

There was no trail this time. But Ah Sahm moved easily down the slippery surfaces and across the narrow ledges. Cord hurried after him, causing miniature landslides as he scrambled and jumped down the steep slopes of sand and gravel. Ah Sahm finally entered a forest of gnarled, wind-driven trees, and Cord caught up to him.

"I realize you are my hidden teacher," Cord said, "and if I am to be able to survive the next

138

trial, I must be allowed to follow you, and to learn."

"You will not be able to endure it."

"I will!"

"But will I?" Ah Sahm asked. He was still moving fast, his thick bamboo flute touching the ground at intervals.

Cord laughed. After the night's rest and the long meditation, he felt more at ease with himself. "Nothing you can say will ever upset me again. I will stay with you!"

Ah Sahm seemed to snort softly. "My heart was light when I awoke. You have just made it heavy again."

"Tell me why I won't be able to endure it."

"You will not have the patience."

"The patience for what?"

"You will not have the patience to stay in contact with the pattern of events. You will see things and judge them before you know what they mean."

"What things."

The old man shook his head. "You even want to know what things before they have happened? Your impatience is beyond . . ."

"I'll be patient!" Cord said emphatically. "I'll be an empty vessel."

"An empty bladder."

"Even that!"

"That will be less difficult for you. One further condition."

"Anything."

"You must ask nothing about any event. Not until such time as I myself give you an answer."

"To no question?"

Ah Sahm suddenly stopped and faced him. For the first time his voice was hard and commanding. "The event will contain the question!"

Cord was taken aback by the old man's tone. He had no idea what Ah Sahm was talking about, but he quickly responded. "Agreed!"

Ah Sahm resumed his fast pace, but they seemed to be moving to the end of a huge promontory. Ah Sahm reached it a few seconds before Cord, and without breaking his pace, he suddenly disappeared from view. Cord came to an abrupt halt and backed up a pace as he looked over the ledge.

The cliff dropped straight down for two hundred feet; its face was a fluted pattern of eroded granite columns. Ah Sahm, however, seemed to be finding his way with no problems. He disappeared from view a few times, then reappeared considerably farther down.

Without hiking back two or three miles, there was no other reasonable route into the valley. Cord considered the problem for a minute, then dropped to his hands and knees and backed over the edge.

By hanging tightly to niches and narrow columns, he angled his way across the upper face and then searched the rocks below for Ah Sahm. The man finally appeared; he had reached the bottom and he was striding down the fanned-out residue of loose shale beneath the cliff.

Cord gaped at him, then started another traverse that took him to a point midway down the cliff. Being blind was perhaps an advantage, Cord reflected as he turned and took a sharper angle down. If a man couldn't see how precipitous a

140

cliff was, he could take all kinds of risks—making himself look like a fool or a magician.

Ah Sahm was nowhere in sight when Cord reached the bottom. Cord slipped and slid down the shale and then loped into the thick forest of pines. He didn't want to lose the man, but he also didn't want to call out. Asking for help would no doubt bring another series of sarcastic observations from the old man.

He jogged through the forest and finally came to a meadow, but there was still no sign of Ah Sahm. From an outcropping that gave him a view of the larger valley below, he scanned the slopes and the valley floor, still seeing nothing.

Had the man abandoned him again, as he had done in the castle ruins and in the forest with the monkeys? If so, why had he talked about giving Cord answers without Cord asking questions? If Ah Sahm was nowhere to be seen, how was he going to give the answers?

Cord sat down and rested his head against a rock. He was growing weary of riddles. And if mysterious things were going to happen, there seemed no point in his running down mountains and tiring himself out looking for them.

He heard nothing. With his eyes closed and the sun bathing his face, he was thinking about Tara and how she had fallen asleep in his arms that morning. And then a shadow suddenly blotted out the sun.

Cord opened his eyes. Ah Sahm was standing over him, a blinding aura of sunlight outlining his head and shoulders. Cord smiled and sat up. But the man was already striding out across the meadow.

141

IX

From the high rim of the valley they could see the wide river and the ancient ferryboat moored at the bank; but they walked for another hour before they reached it. A withered, toothless old man in tattered clothes was sitting against the mooring post, staring vacantly at them as they approached.

A younger man was fishing from the riverbank a few yards away. He was a huge dunce of a man wearing clothes that seemed several sizes too small for him. He frowned stupidly at Cord and Ah Sahm, and then the frown changed into a broad, mindless grin.

The third member of the family, a fat shrew of a woman, glared suspiciously from in front of a tiny hut farther up the riverbank. She was pounding wet clothing on a rock as if resenting the clothes, the river, the sunny day, and anything else that came into her field of vision.

Ah Sahm walked directly to the old man and seemed to glance at the boat and the punting pole inside it. "What is the fare for the two of us?" he asked.

The ferryman rose wearily and squinted at Cord and then Ah Sahm. "Youth, if you could give it to me," he said. "Health, if you had that to spare. I have neither, and need both."

Ah Sahm nodded as if the request were reasonable. "My pupil has youth, but needs it for a while yet. We both have health, but we owe it to time, who demands a little payment every day."

The ferryman gave Cord an assessing glance. "You don't look as if you have any money."

Ah Sahm's hand dipped through a slot in his robe and came out with a tiny ivory figurine. He held it delicately at the base.

The ferryman looked interested. "Ah, yes," he said and squinted at the figure. "That would be . . ."

"Wait, you old fool!"

The command came from the wife. She dropped the laundry and came thumping down the slope, wiping her hands on her apron. "Let me look at that!"

She snatched the figurine from Ah Sahm's fingers and held it to the light. "Hmph! Where'd you steal it?"

Ah Sahm faced her, his head cocked as if studying her face. "My father gave it to me many years ago when I was a child."

The woman snorted. "A likely story." She

144

handed back the figurine and studied Cord from head to toe. "If you wish to cross the river, swim."

"Stop that!" the ferryman exclaimed. "This is an honest man!"

"Yes, just like you're a good man in bed, you seedless stick." The woman turned back to Ah Sahm. "No money, no transportation."

The ferryman glared at her. "It is my boat! I will decide!"

"Your boat? It is mine and your poor son's."

Father up the riverbank the giant with the fish-pole grinned and nodded.

"Since when is it yours?" the man demanded.

"Since I married you, you ignoramus. Everything you have is mine. Didn't I pay for it with the gift of my body and the blessing of a boy child?"

"The gift you gave me *once* thirty years ago? It is my boat, and it will take them across the river! That is the end of it!"

Cord wondered if they had been having the same argument for thirty years. He also wondered if anybody ever managed to get across the river. "Wait," he said and reached in his pouch. "I have money."

The woman grabbed the two coins before her husband had a chance to reach for them. She bit into each of them, then scowled as if disappointed to find they were not counterfeit.

"Take us," Cord said.

The man sighed and looked at the river. "I am too old and in too much pain to pull you across."

Cord gestured at the dimwitted hulk who was still grinning at them from the riverbank. "Then let him do it!"

145

"My baby is fishing!" the woman said. "He has no time to waste on you."

The boy frowned and slowly shook his head from side to side, agreeing with his mother. Then the mindless grin spread across his face again.

"Are you all mad?" Cord asked.

The ferryman shrugged hopelessly. "Not mad. Married."

The situation was ridiculous. Cord strode off to the boat and climbed in. Ah Sahm quietly followed, his face composed and serene.

"Leave it on the other side," the man shouted. "Someone wanting to cross will bring it back."

The man and his wife watched as Cord poled the boat away from the shore. As quickly as he got it moving the man and wife were arguing again. The son grinned at his parents, then grinned at Cord and Ah Sahm.

"That poor man," Cord groaned.

Ah Sahm stood in the center of the boat, facing the far shore. "He is happy."

"Happy!" Cord snorted. "There's misery in every bone in his body."

"Isn't a happy man one who has no fear of death?"

Cord gave Ah Sahm a skeptical glance. He could imagine nothing worse than being married to a woman like that, or having a slobbering idiot for a son.

"The ferryman not only does not fear death," Ah Sahm sad, "his days are filled with the joy of looking forward to it."

"How can one look forward to death—being a bag of bones like that poor man?"

"The bones are already in you. You will learn to embrace them."

Cord made no comment, and turned all his attention to managing the boat. He could see no sense in Ah Sahm's statement. If happiness were merely a matter of dying, it would be a simple thing to achieve. Sometimes he wondered if Ah Sahm formulated preposterous propositions for the sole purpose of rattling him.

The boat was ancient and unwieldy, and most of Cord's efforts went into preventing it from drifting down the river. When it finally thumped into the far bank, Cord jumped ashore and tied the mooring rope to a worn tree trunk.

Ah Sahm stepped out, but he remained close to the boat, his head lifted as if listening to the water lapping against its sides. Cord waited, puzzled by the man's silence. Then he stared in disbelief.

Ah Sahm's foot lifted straight up from the ground, then darted out in a lightning-fast side kick into the boat. The heavy boards at water level shattered inward in a spray of kindling wood. Water immediately began pouring into the bow.

"Why did you do that?" Cord exclaimed.

Ah Sahm moved casually to the other side of the bow and delivered another powerful kick. This time the boards splintered into a thousand fragments that exploded onto the river. Water rushed in, and the bow slowly settled below the surface. The rear of the boat rose and then it slid completely under in a sucking swirl of bubbles.

"The man wanted to help us!" Cord protested. "Is that how you repay him?"

Ah Sahm was already moving up the trail, his head lifted as if searching the landscape ahead.

"You've destroyed his livelihood," Cord said chasing after him. "He'll be defenseless against that woman now!"

Ah Sahm sighed. "I told you you wouldn't be able to avoid jumping to conclusions."

"What kind of conclusions am I supposed to draw from your doing a thing like that?"

"You have a short memory."

Cord sighed and followed him in silence. A short memory: what did that mean? "You will not have the patience to stay in contact with the pattern of events," Ah Sahm had said. "You will see things and judge them before you know what they mean."

Cord still didn't see the sense in smashing the man's boat. Was it punishment for the man's past crimes? Or by depriving the man of his livelihood, did Ah Sahm hope to help him escape from the shrewish wife and the doltish child?

"The event will contain the question," Ah Sahm had also said.

There was no doubt about that, Cord decided. The event contained many questions.

From the river they passed through fields thick with clover and wildflowers. At a fork in the trail, Ah Sahm took the path on the right, and they were soon in a forest of oaks and sycamores. When they were deep among the trees, Ah Sahm's stride shortened. He seemed to be listening as they walked. Then he made an abrupt turn, strode off the trail and ducked into a thick clump of scrub oak.

Cord stopped and stared at him. Ah Sahm was

down on his hands and knees, almost making himself invisible in the thorny foliage.

"What are you doing?" Cord asked.

"Hiding."

"I can see that!"

"When why did you ask?"

Cord stared at him for another minute, then looked around the forest. He could see no dangerous beasts. Nor were any highway robbers poised to attack them. "There's nothing here!"

"Not yet," Ah Sahm answered.

Cord listened, but he could hear nothing. "I never thought I'd see you hiding in the bushes."

Ah Sahm's voice was calm and matter-of-fact. "If the string of a bow is always taut, one day the bow will be useless."

Cord smiled, wondering if Ah Sahm was putting on an act to demonstrate another one of his obtuse lessons. Then he frowned and looked farther along the trail. A distant rumbling—no more than a rhythmic hum—seemed to come from that direction.

The trail curved gently downward for a quarter of a mile and then curved off. Cord watched the curve as the sounds grew louder.

A cloud of dust was slowly rising. Then Cord recognized the rumbling as the sound of galloping horses. A moment later he saw them coming out of the trees—one, two, then four horsemen. Then another four. There were at least a dozen of them.

Ah Sahm called out sadly from the bushes. "They have seen you."

They were a fierce-looking band. Some of the riders had leather helmets with curved animal horns flaring away at the front. Others wore chain mail and heavy gauntlets, and had strips of hammered metal covering their noses and chins. All were brandishing weapons—heavy Turkish swords, or bows and arrows that were strung and ready for battle. The horses were wild-looking animals with bulging eyes and flying manes. They were lathered and snorting, but they were being driven at full speed, their riders snarling and screaming as if consumed with blood lust.

Cord stood transfixed, his heart suddenly high in his throat. Were the riders coming for him and Ah Sahm? Or was there some other enemy nearby? In the bushes, Ah Sahm was moving now, squeezing deeper into the underbrush. Cord stared at him, then gasped as an arrow flicked past his ear and *thunked* solidly into the tree just behind. He turned and ran, plowing into the brush behind Ah Sahm.

The horsemen were fanning out as they came closer. Snarling voices echoed through the forest. Then tree branches were snapping, horses were rearing and snorting, and the pounding of hoofs seemed to be everywhere.

Cord had lost sight of Ah Sahm. Ahead of him, the thorny brush grew thicker and almost impenetrable. On his hands and knees, he scrambled out from under it and then dove behind the protection of three closely grouped trees.

A swarthy man with tangled hair down to his shoulders was swinging a sword from one side of his saddle to the other, hacking at the brush Cord had just left. The horse reared and circled back, and with an angry yank at the reins, the man straightened it again. He jammed his spurs into the flanks, and the horse charged in again, this time crashing through the bushes.

Cord moved to the side of the trees, ready. When the horse and rider flashed past, he leaped high in the air to deliver a jumping front kick. At the pinnacle of the jump, his foot lashed out and his instep caught the rider squarely under the chin. Cord felt the snap of a vertebra, and the man tumbled backwards from the saddle as the horse thundered on.

On his feet again, Cord crouched in front of the trees, one hand touching the ground. An arrow tore past his head and slammed into one of the tree trunks, and once again he dove into the brush. This time he squeezed under the thick growth and scrambled deeper into the woods. Then he stopped, hiding himself in another patch of brush.

He still could not see Ah Sahm. Ahead of him a small wooden hut stood in the center of a clearing. A woman and three small children were racing for the hut, being pursued by a screaming, sword-swinging horseman.

Cord rose, ready to go to their assistance. But the three children and then the woman flew past a stone wall and disappeared in the hut before the horseman reached them.

The horseman galloped past the wall and circled the house, laughing, swinging his sword, then reared his horse in front of the door. He finally lowered the animal's head and gave it a sharp kick in the flanks. The horse's rear hooves shot out and crashed against the stone wall. Stones exploded in the air, and a portion of the wall tumbled in on itself. The horseman roared with glee, wheeled the big animal around, and with another sharp kick sent him flying over the wall.

Behind him, Cord could still hear angry shouts and the sound of swords hacking at the brush. As he looked back, another arrow whipped past within inches of his chest. Thirty feet away, the horseman had already brought another arrow from his quiver and was stringing it across the bow. In one movement, Cord dipped into his pouch and whirled forward, letting a *shurken* fly. The dart buried itself in the man's windpipe just as he raised the bow. Eyes wide, the horse lifted its front legs and bolted forward. A low branch slammed into the rider's mid-section, sending him sprawling to the ground.

Cord ran to his left, away from the sounds of the other horsemen. He was moving around the perimeter of the clearing, keeping himself hidden in the trees as much as possible. He finally reached an area with a dense growth of underbrush, and he plunged in, squeezing into the deepest part.

He breathed heavily, at the same time listening to determine which way the horsemen might be going. The men were still shouting, and four or five of them still seemed to be hacking at the brush. But Cord was a good distance away now. He wriggled forward to a position where he could see the little hut again.

There were no longer any horsemen in the clearing. The woman had closed the door, and now she was hurriedly closing the window shutters.

Cord glanced at the far side of the clearing and then caught his breath.

Ah Sahm was coming out of the forest. He was walking almost casually toward the hut, as if on an afternoon stroll. Cord couldn't believe it. How could the man be so stupid? Surely he could hear all the mad screaming in the forest behind him.

Ah Sahm had reached the stone wall now. He seemed to study it for a minute. Then he leaned his bamboo staff against the wall and went off to retrieve one of the stones the horse had kicked away. He brought it back and fitted it in place. Then he shifted it and wedged it in more securely.

Cord looked off at the forest where the horsemen were still shouting. Then he scrambled out of the brush and loped across the clearing.

"In God's name, are you crazy? Why do you have to pick a time like this to make amends?"

Ah Sahm was bringing another stone back to the wall. He turned his head toward Cord for a moment, but walked on past.

Cord glanced uneasily at the woods. "You're feeling guilty because you kicked in the ferryman's boat," he said, "so now you're committing suicide!"

Ah Sahm carefully fitted the rock into place. "You're not only foolish, you can't keep a promise."

"What promise?"

Ah Sahm moved off for another rock. "In the forest with the monkeys, you told me you were going to cut off your tongue and put it in your pouch."

153

Cord stared incredulously as the man brought the rock back and wedged it in with the others. Then a shrieking cry of discovery came from the direction of the woods.

A horseman was poised at the edge of the clearing, his heavy sword lifted high in the air. A second and then a third horseman joined him. With wild battle cries, they all spurred their horses and charged.

Ah Sahm straightened slowly from the wall. With a stone the size of an orange resting easily in his hand, he stood perfectly still for a minute, listening. Then the arm whipped through an underhanded arc and the stone was gone.

Galloping at full speed, the lead horseman had his sword lifted and was about to hack downward when the stone thudded into his chest. For an instant he appeared to be frozen in place, a look of disbelief in his eyes. Then the sword was spinning in the air and the rider was gone from his horse.

Ah Sahm took a short step forward, his hand lifted high over his head. Then the spinning sword was in his grip and with no seeming effort he swung it through a flat semicircle. The second rider screamed and dropped his sword. He grabbed his side, and blood gushed through his fingers and drenched his leg as the horse galloped on across the clearing.

The third rider had veered off, chasing Cord back toward the woods, closing the gap with each snorting lunge of his big horse. Cord flew across the grass, angling one way and then the other. Then he spotted what he was looking for.

As he plunged into the forest he quickly grabbed the upper trunks of two young trees, bending them almost to the ground.

The horseman eased his mount as he reached the edge of the clearing. Then he lifted his sword and gave the animal a hard kick. The horse crashed blindly forward, trampling brush and crashing through tree branches. At the last moment Cord released the bent treetops. One of them struck the horse squarely on the snout. The animal stumbled, caught himself, and then fell again, sprawling into the brush. The rider flew from the saddle, eyes wide, arms outstretched, and slammed into the dirt ten feet beyond the horse.

Cord was straddling the man's back almost as quickly as he landed. With a quick punch to the back of the head, he snapped the man's neck.

Cord came to his feet and looked quickly at the horse. The animal was puffing and snorting, kicking wildly in an attempt to right itself. Finally the legs found the earth and the huge body rose. The head shook and the animal stared wildly at Cord for a minute. Then it wheeled around and galloped deeper into the woods.

Cord hurried back to the edge of the clearing. He could still hear angry shouts in the trees, but there were no longer any horses in the clearing. One of the riders was lying near the stone wall, his face buried in the dirt. The other was slumped in the grass at the far side of the hut, his left side a mass of red. Cord looked from one to the other, and then stared at the hut.

Ah Sahm was back at work, once more stacking

rocks in the wall. Cord hurried across, keeping one eye on the forest.

It seemed clear that Ah Sahm was going to keep working until every single rock was returned to its original spot. Cord glanced at the woods and at the four or five stones still scattered in the clearing. He hurriedly gathered all of them in his arms and brought them to the wall. As if expecting them, Ah Sahm reached out and one by one carefully set them in their places. Then he stepped back to assess his handiwork.

"The chimney's broken, too," Cord said sarcastically. "We could fix that. And the roof needs mending."

Ah Sahm didn't respond. He brushed the dust from his hands and reached casually for his bamboo staff.

Cord stared off at the woods and quickly touched Ah Sahm's arm. Two more horsemen had spotted them, and another pair was coming out of the forest to join them.

Ah Sahm didn't turn. To Cord's surprise, the old man walked to the end of the wall, and then he was suddenly running at full speed toward the far side of the clearing. Cord bolted after him, running as fast as he could in an effort to keep up.

When they reached the woods they were still fifty yards ahead of the horsemen. Ah Sahm seemed to fly between the trees, making only slight alterations in course as he leaped over logs and bounded across gullies. Behind them, hooves pounded, the horsemen screamed and cursed, and the whole forest seemed to be shattering into splinters.

Ah Sahm suddenly took a sharp turn to the right. He bolted through some brush and headed for what seemed to be an open area. Cord made the same sharp turn, uncertain what the man had in mind. It seemed stupid to let themselves get caught in the open.

They were suddenly out of the forest, and Ah Sahm was scrambling up a rocky slope, leaping from one huge boulder to another. Cord followed, glancing uneasily back at the trees. He jumped to one boulder and then another, then looked up to see in what direction Ah Sahm was going next. Then he stopped and stared at the rocks ahead.

Ah Sahm was sitting down! As if he were finished with his day's business, the man was sitting on a rock, his head leaning against a larger one. Cord glanced quickly over his shoulder and then stared at Ah Sahm again.

He finally realized what Ah Sahm was doing. The way he had positioned himself against the rocks, he was almost invisible. Cord quickly scrambled forward and sat down next to him, arranging himself in a similar position. Then he frowned and looked more closely at Ah Sahm.

His eyes closed, Ah Sahm was breathing easily and deeply, a faint rattle sounding each time he exhaled. He was asleep.

Cord pressed himself closer to the rocks and watched for the horsemen below. They were still shouting and cursing, apparently hacking at everything in sight. After a minute, one of them came out of the forest and reined his horse to a stop at the bottom of the slope. He looked up at the rocks for a minute. Then he looked behind

157

and squinted back into the forest. Finally he gave the horse a kick and charged back into the shadows, once again flailing at the trees and brush.

Cord gave a sigh of relief, then listened as the horsemen worked their way deeper into the woods. Ten minutes later he could hear no more shouting. The horsemen were gone.

Cord eased himself down to a more comfortable position on a small patch of gravel and took a long recovering breath. His heart was finally beating normally again.

Ah Sahm was still sleeping. A tiny bird fluttered down and landed on the rock just above his head. Two more arrived and they darted back and forth pecking at the lichen, keeping a wary eye on Cord. Cord picked up a handful of gravel and let it trickle idly from his fist.

He didn't know what to think about Ah Sahm's behavior. One minute the man fought like a tiger, and the next minute he ran. It didn't make any sense.

Did he want to remain with Ah Sahm? The man was a magician in the martial arts, and his lack of sight sometimes seemed more of an advantage than a handicap. But Cord had some doubts about the man's talents as a teacher. His sinking of the old man's boat seemed like nothing more than a vengeful act of vandalism. And why had he suddenly decided to fix the stone wall while a dozen madmen were screaming for their blood? When he had first sensed the horsemens' approach, he had hidden himself in a bush. Then he seemed to invite them to kill him. The man was crazy.

Cord rose and gazed once more into the forest.

158

Birds were now chattering and flitting from tree to tree, and a thin trail of smoke was rising from the woman's hut.

He would stay, Cord decided. He would stay at least long enough to say good-bye to the man.

X

"I'm thinking of saying good-bye," Cord said when Ah Sahm awakened.

More than an hour had passed, and the blind man had not moved a muscle. Then he suddenly came to his feet and started across the boulders again.

"Good-bye," Ah Sahm said over his shoulder.

Cord followed him to the top of the slope and then down across a broad meadow. Butterflies were flitting from flower to flower, and the clover was thick with bees. Ah Sahm moved lightly across the grass, and the bees seemed to open a path for him.

"I was crazy to believe you were my teacher," Cord said behind him.

"To learn, you have to listen to that which is not spoken."

Cord sighed. It was impossible to talk to the man. No matter what Cord said, Ah Sahm responded with a question or an irrelevant comment. "I'm tired of your riddles. There wasn't any lesson in what happened back there. All I saw was a fool inviting his assassins to kill him."

"You stayed with me."

"I just told you I was crazy."

Ah Sahm shrugged indifferently. "You must learn to control yourself, to look at things as they are, and without prejudice. If you cannot overcome yourself, how can you overcome your trial? The sword cannot cut itself."

Cord snorted his disgust. "And you can't step on the same piece of water twice, and two birds tied together have four wings and can't fly, and the taut bow loses its strength! And now the sword can't cut itself!"

"Your memory is improving."

"But my knowledge is not."

"Good-bye," Ah Sahm said.

Cord looked sharply at the back of the man's head. "Good-bye?"

"A path and a gateway have no meaning or use once the objective is in sight."

Cord laughed. "And a horse has no udders, and a cow can't whinny, and up is down and sideways is straight ahead."

There seemed to be a smile on Ah Sahm's face as he turned from the meadow and began a long climb toward a forested mountainside.

Cord squinted up at the peaks rising above the trees and wondered what the man had in mind now. Ah Sahm seemed to change directions for no apparent reason. Did he have some destination in mind, or did he merely shift with the wind and let it take him wherever it chose?

"A path and a gateway have no meaning or use once the objective is in sight." The observation made some sense, but what did it mean in relation to Cord? Was he now supposed to understand that the objective was in sight? Was it in the forest? Or the top of the mountain?

It was neither place. Once he reached the forest, Ah Sahm turned again. He followed the wooded slope around the mountainside to a high shoulder and then dropped into the next valley. He strode through the meadows at a good pace, and then continued until they suddenly emerged on a broad beach.

Ah Sahm still did not stop. The sun was almost touching the western horizon, but he took no notice of it. He walked steadily along the wet sand, his footprints slowly dissolving behind him. Rocky outcroppings and pieces of driftwood sometimes blocked their path. Ah Sahm seemed to anticipate the obstacles; he picked his way through the driftwood, and effortlessly stepped over the rocks.

Far ahead Cord could make out a cluster of small fires on the beach. As they drew closer he saw a fishing boat drawn up on the sand. The fishermen were spreading small octopuses on drying racks, and farther up from the shore women were preparing meals over the fires.

Five or six ragged children suddenly broke loose and came running to Cord and Ah Sahm. They held out their hands for money, or sweets, or anything else that might be offered. Some giggled and danced around them. Others shouted and cajoled, tugging at Cord's arms. Once they noticed Ah Sahm's sightless eyes, they didn't bother him.

Cord smiled and jostled the hair of a couple of the boys. He shrugged and opened his hands, showing them he had nothing to give.

On the sand between the boat and the campfires a boy of about thirteen stood watching Cord and Ah Sahm approach. He was a beautiful boy with light, silken hair that flowed down to his shoulders. A woman was brushing it for him, her mouth tense as she carefully guided each stroke. The boy seemed irritable and impatient. When the brush momentarily snagged one of his tresses, he jerked his head away and gave the woman a look of disgust.

When they were a short distance from the boy, Ah Sahm stopped and lifted his head, apparently sensing something about what was going on.

Cord glanced at the fishermen and back to the boy, wondering how anybody in such a rough and battle-scarred group of people could have produced such a child. The boy held himself like a prince; he kept his chin lifted and his wide, almond-shaped eyes regarded everything with mild contempt. He belonged on a throne, or a pedestal somewhere, and no one seemed more conscious of it than he did.

A gap-toothed fisherman broke away from his work and got a small piece of meat from the cooking pots. As if to tell Ah Sahm and Cord that he was responsible for the masterpiece, he smiled at them and handed the meat to the boy.

The boy's mouth tightened as he took the meat

and chewed it for a few seconds. Then he scowled and flung it into the sand. With an impatient gesture, he broke away from the hairbrushing and strode haughtily over to Ah Sahm and Cord. He lifted his chin and thrust out an open hand to receive their offering.

The other children backed away as if acknowledging the young man's prerogatives, and the fishermen and all the women stopped working and watched, none of them seeming to breathe. Cord smiled to himself, wondering if Ah Sahm would hand over his small figurine—or if he would offer the boy some words of wisdom.

Ah Sahm's hand moved, but it did not go into the slot of his robe. It came upward and chopped across so fast, Cord wasn't sure at first if it had moved at all.

The crowd gasped as the boy's head snapped back. Then a thin line of blood appeared across his cheek and nose. For a moment the boy also seemed not to realize what had happened. The eyes widened, and the expression that only a few seconds earlier had been arrogant and imperious was suddenly fearful and desperate. His nose was rapidly swelling into a grotesque shape, and blood gushed from the nostrils. The boy's hand came to his face and he cried out. Then he ducked his head and ran sobbing to the woman with the hairbrush.

Cord was shocked. At first he couldn't believe Ah Sahm had struck the child. Then he was certain the father and all the other fishermen were going to come at them with clubs and harpoons. The people appeared to be stunned, but no one moved. The children gaped from Ah Sahm to the wounded prince, and the women and fishermen stared silently at the boy's parents.

The boy's mother opened her arms to him, and the man who had given him the meat rested a hand on the boy's shoulder. As the boy whimpered, the man patted his shoulder with an awkward movement, and then he gazed evenly at Ah Sahm. There was no anger or resentment in the weary eyes. The man simply stared for a minute and then sighed as if a great burden had just been lifted from his shoulders.

As though nothing had happened, Ah Sahm moved calmly past the boat and resumed his walk along the beach. Then, one by one, the women and fishermen quietly turned back to their work.

Cord wasn't sure what to do. He was embarrassed, and he was angry that Ah Sahm had committed such an unfriendly act. With only the children watching him now, he walked past the boat and struck out after Ah Sahm. When he caught up to him, he grabbed roughly for the blind man's shoulder.

Instead of whirling Ah Sahm around, Cord's hand grasped nothing but air. Ah Sahm stood calmly facing Cord.

Cord stared at the man. Ah Sahm's head was slightly tilted, and his body was in the same relaxed, almost listless posture with which he had faced the monkey and the thugs in the castle.

Cord eased back a step. "Why?!!" he demanded in a harsh, almost choking voice.

Ah Sahm said nothing. His head shifted a fraction, and he seemed to be gazing at something behind Cord. Cord looked back.

The women and the fishermen were now gathering around the boy and his parents. Some were smiling—even grinning—and they seemed far more animated than when Cord and Ah Sahm had first arrived. The boy still had his head on his mother's shoulder, and the father was casually patting him on the back.

Cord turned back to Ah Sahm, all the frustrations suddenly rising within him. "This time I'm going!"

Ah Sahm sighed and slowly walked away. "You must stop making promises."

"This isn't a promise. It's a decision." In spite of his words, Cord once more stepped out after the man. He fully intended to separate from him, but not until he had some answers.

"Now that I'm free of you," Cord announced, "I'm free to ask questions. Explain yourself! What did you mean by kicking the ferryman's boat?"

Ah Sahm stopped. Instead of facing Cord, he turned the sightless eyes to the setting sun. "Of the two of us," he said, "you are the blind one. Blinded by the things you see and hear. You *think,* therefore you stand apart from the things you try to understand."

Cord glared at him. "I want an *answer,* not a dissertation."

Ah Sahm nodded as if agreeing. "I damaged the boat because if I hadn't, the war party would have confiscated it. The horsemen would have crossed the river, and the old man would have been killed."

The answer was reasonable if one presumed Ah Sahm had knowledge of the approaching horsemen. If he did not, the answer was nothing more than after-the-fact rationalization.

167

"How did you know the war party was coming?" Cord challenged. "Did you hear them?"

"No," Ah Sahm said. "Does that properly answer a question with an answer?"

"The wall," Cord said. "Why did you stop to repair it?"

"When the horse kicked the wall and dislodged the stones, a hidden bag of coins was left exposed. I repaired the wall so the horsemen wouldn't find the bag and steal it. If the coins had been taken, the widow and her three children would have been left without means."

"You couldn't *see* the bag. How did you know it was there? Did you smell it?"

"No."

Cord took a long breath. Even when the man answered questions he said nothing. "All right," Cord said, "but the boy! Explain the boy!"

"The boy," Ah Sahm said as if quietly tasting the word.

"Yes, the boy. You mutilated him! You broke his nose. A beautiful boy!"

Ah Sahm nodded. "He was too beautiful. He was already a tyrant. He would have grown worse. I freed his parents from their subjugation to his beauty."

"You didn't see his face, or even touch him. How did you know what he looked like? Did you sense it?"

"No. But I freed the parents, and the boy as well. And now, I free you of me." He turned and moved rapidly along the beach, his robes flaring behind.

Cord frowned, considering Ah Sahm's answers. He was probably right about the boy's beauty making him a tyrant. But that could be more his parents' fault than his. And now that the boy was maimed, would the parents revenge themselves for his previous arrogance and contempt? If so, would Ah Sahm return some day and break their noses, too? Cord shook his head, unable to arrange the possibilities into a sensible pattern.

Ah Sahm was far down the beach now, still moving fast. Cord watched him for a minute and then broke into a run.

"I'm not finished yet!" he shouted when Ah Sahm was within hearing distance.

Ah Sahm continued the fast pace, and Cord hurried along behind him. "You didn't *hear* the war party," he said, "and you didn't *smell* the bag of coins, and you didn't *sense* the boy's beauty. So how did you know? I want an explanation!"

"If I didn't sense or smell or hear, how did I know?" Ah Sahm asked.

Cord strode along in silence. "I've got it!" he finally said. "You knew all those things because you've passed through here before!"

Ah Sahm stopped so abruptly a plume of sand sprayed across the beach. Cord also stopped, and Ah Sahm wheeled and took two swift steps back to him.

"How many times?" Ah Sahm demanded.

Cord gaped at him, mouth open, not certain he understood the question. Then his head jerked back as he felt Ah Sahm's hand smack across his cheek.

It was a Zen monk's slap; the jarring surprise that knocked loose the entrenched and restricting thought patterns. Lo Tzu had used it many times on Cord, and the expected result was that he would see and understand without relying on the habitual and rigid steps of syllogistic logic.

Ah Sahm was no longer standing in front of him. He was now a quarter of a mile farther up the beach, gliding smoothly past the driftwood, a tiny figure in the gathering darkness.

Cord understood part of what Ah Sahm was trying to tell him. He was pointing out that Cord was asking that all questions be answered in a logical manner, complete with concrete evidence that was consistent with the temporal world. And it was Cord's insistence on such so-called proof that was blinding him. All the mysterious things that had occurred were not events presented for Cord's dissection and analysis. They were for him to accept as reality, and for him to contemplate without questioning.

Cord touched his face and then thoughtfully rubbed his jaw as he walked slowly along the beach. "Of the two of us," Ah Sahm had said, "you are the blind one. Blinded by the things you see and hear. You *think*, therefore you stand apart from the things you try to understand."

Cord understood what Ah Sahm demanded of him. But he did not understand what it would lead to.

The tide was coming in. Small waves broke and tumbled into the shore, rushing gently up the wet slope and across his feet.

Cord smiled as he watched the water hiss and gurgle and slide back into the sea. You cannot step on the same piece of water twice.

The same thing could be said about Ah Sahm. Or more accurately, you could not step on Ah

170

Sahm *once*. He was as elusive as a piece of water . . . and as stubborn as a man in a barrel of oil.

Cord stopped and gazed out at the ocean, watching the dark tumble of surf. Then he strode into the water, pushing forward until he had reached waist level. Breathing deeply, he closed his eyes and stood perfectly still, one hand dropped below the surface.

He concentrated, his submerged hand open, keeping himself braced against the small waves that swirled past. For several minutes he felt nothing. Then a slimy surface brushed lightly against his fingers. He held them open, waiting, and once again he felt it. In one motion, he closed the fingers and lifted his hand from the water.

A three-foot-long string of seaweed dangled from his fingers. He sighed wearily and trudged back to the beach.

He accepted everything. He accepted Ah Sahm's knowledge of the approaching war party, and his actions in destroying the ferryman's boat. He accepted Ah Sahm's knowkedge of the bag of coins in the wall, and he accepted Ah Sahm's recognition of a tyrant in the beautiful boy. Ah Sahm knew about these things solely because they were true. He did not need eyes to see them, nor did the facts have to be communicated to him in any understandable way. Solely because the truths existed, Ah Sahm was aware of them. The same was true of the fish in the stream, the men attacking him in the ruins, and the horsemen attacking him in the clearing.

Cord breathed deeply, his upturned palms resting on his knees. He repeated the propositions

171

over and over again, willing himself to believe them. Then he let his thoughts settle, the muddy pool of his mind slowly clearing as the silt and debris drifted to the bottom.

Ligntning did not strike. Nor did any great truths rise in the darkness and illuminate the mysteries. After an hour of meditation he rose and looked out at the sea.

For some reason he was restless. He had climbed onto the rocky cliff to think about Ah Sahm and the events of the day. But he seemed unable to concentrate, or to address himself wholly to the questions.

He looked up at the stars, and then at the cliff rising another fifty feet above him. He finally moved upward, working his way along ledges and up the eroded columns. At the top of the cliff, broad grassy slopes rose high above the shore. Without thinking or questioning himself about the direction he should take, he headed north, following the line of the sea.

XI

Cord followed the sea for several miles. At length the bluffs flattened into arid, desert-like terrain, and the water along the shore was warm and still.

A massive shadow loomed larger and larger on the horizon. When he was within a mile of it, Cord found huge blocks of granite strewn over the beach and into the shallower water. It was as if some ship, or fleet of ships, had been unloading building materials when the operation was interrupted by a battle, or perhaps a devastating storm.

The structure facing the beach appeared to be a fortress of some kind. Parts of it had crumbled completely, leaving sections of walls, and lonely towers that rose like black voids against the starry sky.

173

Cord moved up the beach to broad, sand-covered steps that took him to an open courtyard. The area was overgrown with weeds and strewn with the rubble of collapsing walls. There appeared to be an amphitheater off to the side, and a partially standing aqueduct was silhouetted against the sky. He moved through a broad archway into a smaller courtyard where he stood listening for a minute.

He could hear the rustling of mice, and from somewhere overhead three or four birds swooped across from one wall to the other. They chattered for a moment and then seemed to settle themselves.

Several doors opened into the courtyard. Cord moved through the largest of them and found himself in a dark corridor. He moved cautiously, stumbling several times, and finally was in the open again.

The walls around him were crumbling and dusty. He followed one of the larger ones, turning several corners. Then he stopped, listening again. There were no sounds now. On either side of him were dark, unidentifiable shadows, and he had the feeling of some ominous presence.

Was it his imagination, or were the stars overhead less bright than when he looked at them from the beach? He edged back a few paces, but suddenly found a wall behind him. He felt along the stones, first in one direction, then the other. There seemed to be no opening.

It was impossible. He was certain of the direction he had come from. Or had he become disoriented? He moved forward again, more cautiously now, all his senses alerted. Then he suddenly caught his breath and froze.

From very nearby, a bloodcurdling scream shattered the silence. It seemed to come from something part beast and part human, and Cord wasn't certain whether it came from the left or right. He dropped a hand into his pouch and clutched a dart, at the same time crouching slightly, ready to move.

He saw it for only an instant—a black and white form that seemed to materialize in the air to his right. Then it was coming at him, like some huge, snarling animal leaping through space.

Cord's reaction was purely instinctive. He threw himself backward, at the same time lifting a protective arm. The beast was in front of him, and then it was gone before he could release the dart.

He had felt only the rush of air. It was as if the thing had leaped from a high wall, bounded once in front of him, and leaped out of sight again.

Cord held himself still, listening, watching for the thing to reappear. Then he felt something warm trickling down the bridge of his nose. He touched his brow, then his forehead. There was an open wound just under his hairline, a long slashing cut. Then he felt the stinging line of pain down the side of his arm and across the front of his thighs.

Somehow, in that split second, the animal or apparition, or whatever it was, had clawed him. With one movement, it had sliced open a semi-circular line of flesh from his head to his legs.

Cord fingered the dart and searched the high

175

shadows surrounding him. But once again everything was silent. He waited another half-minute, then moved forward again.

At the back of the fortress, he found a pond. A narrow trickle of water meandered into the area and formed a boggy field of grass. After he had cleansed his wounds, he found enough wood scraps to build a fire.

He sat close to the flames, examining the sharp cuts along his arm. They had not pierced deeply enough to injure the muscles, but the skin was sliced as cleanly as if it had been done by a razor. He packed mud around the cuts. Then he listened as several bullfrogs croaked somewhere in the shadows.

He rose, listening closely to the sounds. From the fire he moved into the shadows and circled broadly around the bog. When the frogs were between him and the fire he crept stealthily forward. He grabbed one frog from behind and then grasped the legs of another as it leaped to escape. A minute later he had a third. He dropped them all in his pouch and carried them back to the fire.

Using strands of long grass, he braided three-foot-long cords. He tied one to the leg of each frog, and using heavy rocks to secure them, he placed the frogs in a triangular pattern twenty feet from the fire.

The animals leaped and twisted and struggled, but they finally settled down to croaking again. Cord listened for awhile and then stretched out by the fire with a dart in each hand. As long as the croaking continued, he knew nothing would sneak up on him.

As he closed his eyes he thought about Ah Sahm again. Considering the way they had parted, he presumed he would never see the man again. But he wondered if Ah Sahm knew where Zetan could be found. And with Ah Sahm's skills as a martial artist, why hadn't he defeated Zetan and become the Keeper of the Book? Or was Zetan an even greater fighter?

Weariness finally seeped through his body and reached his brain. With one arm thrown to the side and the other resting on his chest, he drifted into an uneasy sleep. In his dreams there were monkey-men galloping after him on wild horses, and the man in the oil barrel was laughing and swinging a big sword. His muscles twitched and jumped as he envisioned himself running through meadows and scampering up cliffs. Then the sounds of a flute soothed his restlessness. He was in a grassy field, and the sun was warming his face. He lay down to rest, and frogs were softly croaking all around him.

Silence awakened him. He sat bolt upright, his darts ready, and searched the bog in every direction. In the misty darkness he could see nothing. To the east a broad streak of gray marked the horizon. The sun would be coming up soon.

He started to ease back, but a small movement in the bushes far to his left stopped him. He stared at the bush, then came quickly to his feet, a *shurken* ready.

The bushes moved again. Then a second shadow suddenly materialized. For a moment it was stationary. Then it darted past him so fast he wasn't sure if he had seen it or not. He turned sharply and stared at the bushes into which the thing had disappeared. Then the form was coming at him again. It came low, and then it was suddenly six feet in the air, issuing the same hideous scream.

His heart now in his throat, Cord threw one and then the other dart. As quickly as he let them fly, he knew they had missed, and he pivoted and kicked straight out at the flying creature.

The kick met its target, but it had no more effect than as if he had kicked at a charging buffalo. The impact slammed him tumbling backwards, and he quickly whirled to the side as the creature tore past. He came instantly to his feet, ready, but once again the beast was gone.

He stood perfectly still, watching the shadows. Then he felt fresh blood seeping down his forehead. He had more cuts, and now a thin line of pain burned down his other arm and across his thighs. The thing had duplicated the injuries of the first attack, except this time on the opposite side.

Cord touched his thigh and realized he was gripping something in his fist. It was hair; a thick tuft of black hair. He looked up and once more saw the shadowy creature. But this time it was bounding away into the brush. "What are you?" he shouted.

The thing disappeared in the mist.

Cord looked once more at the hairs. They were long and fine, almost silken. He stared at them, wondering, then he looked off into the darkness. "Or does it matter what you are?" he said softly. "Or what shape you have?"

He turned slowly and surveyed the surrounding

brush. "Whether or not your hair is coarse or fine
—it makes no difference!"

A chill ran down his spine. He was afraid, but
he was also excited, eager to get on with it.
"Death!" he shouted. "Come back! Do I have to
die to meet Zetan? Then I am ready! Are you still
there?"

The bogs were silent.

Cord smiled ironically as he moved around the
clearing and untied the frogs. The time and place
would be up to the creature. He watched the frogs
hop away, then studied the bushes again.

"Of course you are here!" he said. "Death is always present. Why was I afraid? Death was already sitting by my side when I was born!"

It was clear now, so clear he felt foolish at not
having realized it long ago. It was something he
knew *about,* but had never *known.*

"Death!" he shouted. "Listen! What can you
take from me which is not yours sooner or later?"

He listened, but the bog seemed extraordinarily
silent now—as if the beast was also listening. Cord
laughed and picked up his pouch. He crossed
the clearing and climbed the hill above the fortress. At the top he sat beneath a cedar tree and
closed his eyes in meditation. He had no fears
now; he was looking forward to the battle. He
strove only to empty his mind of all the past fears
and doubts.

When he rose again, the sun was well above the
horizon. He studied the valley below, where the
little stream trickled down toward the fortress.
Then he loped down the hill and crossed to a thick
stand of bamboo plants.

Feeling buoyant and sure of himself, he cut a bamboo stalk and carefully carved himself a dart. When it was finished, he hefted it lightly for balance, then added dirt to one of the hollow compartments.

He spent the rest of the morning practicing with the *shurken*. With one movement he lifted two of the darts from his pouch and gripped them in the palm of his hand, ready to throw.

Expert handling of the *shurken* was an art that Cord had never practiced enough to become a master. But the lightning speed of the beast that attacked him required equal speed on his part. He had improved enough so that he was confident he could release the two darts simultaneously. But he was not certain he could kill the beast. He tried again, whirling left and then right. Then he stopped suddenly, listening.

The sound of Ah Sahm's flute was drifting through the valley. It seemed distant at first. But then, as if carried by the wind, the notes seemed to pass close to Cord's ear.

"The bones in you are already there," Ah Sahm's voice repeated quietly. "You will learn to embrace them."

Cord turned sharply to the stand of bamboo plants. Then he whirled again and searched the surrounding hills. Ah Sahm was nowhere in sight.

"I do embrace them!" Cord called out. "I *have* learned."

He listened, but neither Ah Sahm's voice nor the flute responded. He finally gazed in the direction of the fortress—at the unseen beast he knew was stalking him.

"I have been seeking the truth," he said aloud,

"and the truth has been seeking me. I have been seeking death, and death has been seeking me. We have met at last, face to face, and there is no fear. I am prepared. I am at peace."

He waited, listening again, but he could hear only the soft rustling of the wind through the bamboo. He finally turned and resumed his journey, still following the line of the sea.

At dusk, the wind rose. At first there were only tentative gusts, short spurts that buffeted the leaves and sent waves rippling across the surface of the sea. But the gusts grew steadily stronger and more frequent, and by nightfall Cord was striding into a relentless gale. He pushed onward, too exhilarated to feel any weariness from the long day of traveling. He shouted occasionally, challenging the beast to show himself, but the words were torn from his lips and swept away with the howling wind.

He had crossed a river and was moving through a dense growth of jungle when he finally sensed the presence. In the tangled darkness of trees and vines, there seemed to be an even darker shadow lurking nearby. He stopped and listened, all his senses alert as he studied the small clearing.

For a full minute he waited. The heavy foliage above him almost blotted out the stars, and it was hard to tell what might be lying in wait. Then, at the far edge of the clearing, a shadow moved a few inches. A low snarl sounded, and Cord stiffened, his hand in his pouch.

As the beast suddenly leaped, Cord lifted his arm, ready. Then he caught himself as the thing landed several yards in front of him. It was almost as if the animal were playing games with him—amusing itself by delaying the kill for a while.

For the first time, Cord had a clear look at his adversary. It was in the form of a man, but had the long claws and the head of a panther. Its eyes glistened like black fire, and the two eyeteeth curved several inches below its lips. For a moment it gazed silently at him: the superior animal confident of victory. Then the low snarl sounded almost like a laugh as it rose and came slowly forward. The front claws were now lifted, glistening like sharpened blades in the pale light.

Cord lowered the darts and held himself motionless, his gaze fixed on the flashing eyes. His heart was thudding heavily against his breastbone, and yet he felt no fear. The animal was *death*, and whatever form it chose to take, he no longer felt any need to run from it. He smiled, keeping his head high.

"Why are you so ugly?" he asked.

The eyes narrowed and the claws jerked in a threatening gesture as the animal came slowly forward again.

"Or do you have a different face for every man?" Cord said.

The jaws opened, and a bloodcurdling scream split the air. The animal darted forward with two quick steps. Once again Cord lifted the darts—then he tossed them into the dirt a few feet in front of the snarling animal.

For the first time, the panther-man stopped snarling. The eyes widened and the beast's head snapped back as if Cord had struck it in the face. Then, with an angry scream, the animal lunged.

Cord stood his ground. His arms outspread, he

took the full impact of the animal's charge. Then he locked his arms around the hairy body.

The panther-man continued to shriek and snarl. It swung one way and then the other, struggling to free itself from Cord's embrace.

"Kill me," Cord commanded. "There is no escape from you."

The animal lifted its arms, ready to plunge the long claws into Cord's back.

Cord held on, tightening his grip. "Now, or in a month, or in a year, you will take me."

A low growl came from the animal's throat as it slowly lowered the claws. Then, with a violent twist, it wrenched itself free and stepped back into a half-crouch. The eyes now glittered with anger and frustration.

Cord smiled, knowing he had won. "Shall I whimper first?" he asked. "And cry for help? Shall I go to my knees? Are you waiting for fear to freeze my heart before you carve it out?"

The animal was panting heavily now. Without a cringing, terrified victim, the sport was gone. The glittering eyes dropped from Cord and for a moment seemed to search the ground on both sides of him. Then, crab-like, the beast slowly retreated, the long claws brushing along the ground.

"Come any time, welcome guest," Cord said.

The beast stared at him from the far edge of the clearing. The head nodded as if it were acknowledging the invitation and looking forward to a time when it might find Cord in more fearful circumstances. Then, as if to remind Cord of its ferociousness, the animal bared its teeth and lifted a threatening claw over its head. At almost the same instant it seemed to dissolve into thin air.

Cord gazed at the empty spot, his heart now beating easily. The jungle was silent, and there were no longer any fears or doubts in his mind. He heaved a long sigh and strode easily across the clearing. He smiled as he heard a final threatening shriek far behind him.

XII

Late in the night Cord stopped at a river and bathed himself. Then he meditated until morning. At sunrise he followed a narrow path that paralleled the coast and then took him farther north through thick forests of pines and cedar trees.

Somewhere a drum was beating, a slow, ponderous thumping that grew steadily louder as the day passed. The sound seemed to be moving in the same direction he was, but at a slightly slower speed. When darkness finally came, he turned from the path and threaded his way through the heavy growth toward the sea.

A mass of tents and several dozen campfires were spread along the beach. Cord paused at the edge of the forest and then dropped down the sandy slopes to the encampment.

With all the shouting, laughter, and dancing

185

girls, there was no doubt that it was the same caravan Cord had encountered on the desert. The same sentry who had watched him enter the encampment before now smiled as if he were an old friend.

The clowns, slave girls, and tumblers were still running among the tents in their endless pursuit of pleasure. For a moment a flickering of anger rose in Cord as he made his way through the crowd. But the anger was directed mostly at himself, and the foolish things he had done the last time he had met Changsha.

Just as he had found him before, the big Turk was once again massaging a black bull, kneading the big animal's neck and shoulders. Cord stood and watched him for a minute, then moved casually forward.

Changsha gave him a quick glance and then squinted as if not quite believing his eyes. "What's this? Cord? Yes, Cord! Ah . . . the interesting young man I entertained in the wilderness."

Changsha's smile faltered as Cord gazed silently back at him. "The very same Cord," he said. He leaned on the bull's back and regarded Cord thoughtfully. "No . . . not the same."

"Not quite," Cord said.

Changsha smiled and turned back to the bull. "But you're still looking for the same . . ."

"Zetan."

"Ahh, yes. Zetan."

The Turk nodded and opened his hand. He gazed at it for a moment, then, in a lightning-fast movement, he closed the fist and drove it into the back of the bull's skull. The animal's legs splayed out beneath it, and the heavy body dropped instantly to the ground. Changsha smiled and watched as six servants rushed forward and dragged off the inert body. "Zetan," he said and turned back to Cord. "He's very near. Oh, very, very near. All you have to do is pass by me."

"I have no quarrel with you," Cord said.

Changsha grinned. "Amazing. No quarrel with me? But your love, Tara . . . sweet, beautiful, *giving* Tara. Did I not crucify her?"

"No," Cord said quietly.

"No? But I myself, with these two hands . . ."

"No, I—myself—with these two hands. I tried to take her away. I tried to own her. And so I sent her to her death!"

Changsha turned his palms upward and slowly shook his head. "Not the same Cord. Then you do not confront me with hate?"

"No," Cord said. "With disgust."

Changsha shrugged. "Why confront me at all? Join me. Take my hand." He chuckled and gestured easily at the noisy crowd. "I can show you a world where disgust and guilt never exist. With me you'll find no night or day, the sun will never set or rise, and endless pleasures will replace the hours and minutes that now race with you to your death! Come with me!"

"My goal is Zetan," Cord said.

Changsha gazed thoughtfully at him and finally nodded. "Ah, yes . . . Zetan. You will meet me at daybreak. Along the beach."

"And after I pass you, Zetan, is very near?"

"Yes. That I promise you. Your search will then be over."

"Very well," Cord said. "At daybreak. Along the beach."

He strode away without looking back. The frolicking crowd paid no attention as he squeezed through. Once again he saw unattended booths with all kinds of fruits, nuts, and spicy candies. He stopped long enough to fill his pouch and then strode out of the camp.

Could he beat a man who killed bulls with a single punch? Cord felt confident. It was not so much confidence in his ability to beat the big Turk as it was a certainty that he would fight better than he had ever fought before. He had no fear of making any foolish mistakes. He was now in control of himself, and neither the dancing antics of monkeys or the rhythm of drums or the fear of death would distract him.

From the encampment he moved back to the edge of the forest and settled himself in a position overlooking the beach. He felt no tensions or anxieties, and while he ate, he watched the frenzied activities below.

He wondered what Changsha meant when he said Zetan was very near. Was it possible that Zetan and the Book of Wisdom traveled in Changsha's caravan? Or was Changsha Zetan? And if he beat Changsha, would that mean he would take his place and forever travel around the countryside with that circus of debauchery? If the Book of Wisdom advised such an existence, Cord wondered what kind of evidence and reasoning it offered to justify it.

It appeared as though everyone in the camp had now learned of the contest that was to take place at daybreak. All the musicians seemed to be playing at once, and mobs of singing and dancing people were converging on Changsha's huge tent. It looked as if it were going to be one continuous orgy until the sun came up.

Cord closed his eyes and breathed deeply, each breath diminishing the external sounds a little more. His mind was a lake. The incoming streams of distraction were now cut off, and the water was no longer churning. The surface was still and glassy, and very slowly the silt and debris were settling to the bottom. The water was growing clear and transparent. All things were visible.

When Cord awakened, the eastern sky was a narrow streak of flaming red. He gazed vacantly at it for a minute before he realized where he was and what significance the sunrise had. Below him the campfires were burning and the people were already moving toward the huge Persian carpet that had been spread over the sand. Cord rose and stretched, looking up at the last glimmer of stars in the gray sky.

He smiled as he moved down the sandy slope. Would death be waiting among the crowd? If Changsha beat him, would the panther rush gleefully forward to deliver the final blow?

Changsha's musicians, jugglers, and slave girls were there when Cord arrived. Behind them and surrounding the carpet ten deep were all the other caravan members, most of them grinning and laughing, anticipating a lively show. They stepped aside, clearing a path for Cord, and he strode easily through, his mind and body still at peace.

Changsha was already there. He was stripped to the waist, the hard brown muscles glistening with oil. He was grinning, feet apart, hands on his hips, his dark eyes following Cord to the edge of the carpet.

The crowd suddenly went silent as Cord took his position across from the man. He smiled faintly and bowed.

Changsha bowed in return, his broad smile now showing amusement and anticipated pleasure. "The day has broken," he said.

"Yes," Cord answered.

"I do this, Cord, only because you require it."

"Yes," Cord responded. "I know you like to please your guests."

Changsha nodded and came forward. The drums echoed his movements, beginning their slow, monotonous thumping. Cord also came forward, knees slightly bent, head tilted, his hands ready.

Changsha moved slowly from left to right and then left again, carefully studying Cord, searching his defensive stance. Cord instinctively followed the movements, but he was in a far more relaxed posture than in his previous battles. It was a composed alertness, and with no conscious effort he was aware of every shift and turn of Changsha's body. Several times the big Turk's eyes narrowed and he glanced at Cord's face as if giving silent approval to the younger man's smooth and effortless adjustments.

A reedy instrument began to play, and Changsha's arms and hands gracefully followed the rhythm, moving higher and higher as he circled back and forth around Cord.

Cord tried to ignore the sinuous movements. He moved one way and then the other, trying to keep his attention focused solely on the general attitude of Changsha's body. But the hands and fingers were like the dancers in a dazzling ballet, drawing his attention first here, then there. Cord blinked and jerked his head in an effort to break the spell. But he was quickly drawn back into the hypnotic maze. It was the dance of the monkey-man—the entrapment of the projected ego—and Cord found himself unable to break out of the beguiling net.

He took a quick, deep breath and blew it out, crouching slightly lower as he followed Changsha's movements. The music was softer now, almost a whisper, and Cord was suddenly conscious of Tara dancing in front of him, The hands were soft and supple and beckoning. There was warmth and tenderness and the promise of pleasure, and Cord was drawn slowly forward, unable to detach himself from the memory.

The kick came from Cord's right side. At one moment he was moving to the left, following the gently dancing hands. Then the hands were gone, and instead of Tara smiling seductively in front of him, Changsha was at his right side, his foot lashing out at Cord's chest.

Cord threw his head back, at the same time twisting away from the kick. The foot glanced harmlessly off his breastbone, but for an instant he was defenseless, his lower body exposed to an inside punch or a groin kick. He whirled back into position before Changsha could take advantage of the opening. At the same time he tried to shake off the image of Tara and the hypnotic effect of the dancing hands.

More musicians were playing, and the music was growing louder, the drums thudding insistently. Cord blocked the sounds from his mind and concentrated on Changsha, watching closely for an

191

opening. The Turk was weaving and bobbing again, his shoulders rolling and dipping with the beat of the drum. Cord made a quick feint, and then another, but Changsha quickly responded with his own feigned attacks.

Cord backed away for a moment and came back in. Then he stopped short and blinked uncertainly. Was his vision playing tricks on him? Changsha seemed to have split into three separate bodies, all of them dancing to the rhythm of the music. The other two forms were not duplications of Changsha. The one on the left was Jungar, the monkey-man from the caves, and the other was the fanged panther with the glittering eyes of death.

Cord blinked several more times and retreated a half-step. He looked sharply from one to the other and back to Changsha's grinning face, still not sure if he was seeing things. Then a hideous scream came from his left, and Jungar was flying at him, his legs cocked for a double flying kick.

Cord dropped under the first foot and whirled away from the second. When he re-set himself, he quickly braced for an attack from Changsha or the panther-man. But they were both gone. Only the monkey-man was circling him now.

Cord quickly pulled back into his nucleus stance. The crowd was chanting now, their voices roaring with the drumbeats. Cord turned, keeping Jungar always in front of him. The monkey-man danced and gyrated and circled back in the opposite direction. But Cord was in control of himself again. He kept the monkey at bay, turning smoothly with every movement, his gaze fixed coldly on the center of the gyrating figure.

As if aware that his antics were having no effect, the monkey-man suddenly stopped the dance. The eyes darkened, he took a deep breath and charged straight ahead. He feinted left, then right, then whipped his body around as he delivered a fast spin kick. Cord weaved and shifted with the feints, then threw his head to the side when the kick came. He avoided the full impact of the blow. But the whirling foot brushed across his forehead with a stinging slash.

Cord backed away, feeling blood trickle into his eyebrows. The cut he had received from the panther-man had been reopened. He brushed the back of his hand across the wound and quickly positioned himself. Then he blinked uncertainly.

Jungar was gone. In his place, Changsha was grinning, his hands and fingers once more dancing in the air to the rhythm of the music. Cord watched him, this time determined not to be seduced by the hypnotic movements. He followed Changsha through a complete circle and then held himself ready as the big Turk edged forward as if preparing to charge.

The attack came with an explosive leap. Changsha crouched low and then he was suddenly a hairy animal flying at Cord with flashing claws. Cord ducked, dropping a hand to the ground as the rush of wind fled past him. When he pivoted to face the attacker again, the panther-man was once more crouched low. The eyes glittered, and a low snarl came from the throat as he lifted the claws.

Again the animal leaped. This time the claws flashed low, as if the beast expected Cord to duck again. But Cord dived to the side and quickly righted himself, ready for the next lunge.

The panther-man was no longer there. His head swaying from side to side, Changsha was grinning at him, his teeth holding the bamboo dart Cord had carved the day before. In his hand, he was holding two *shurken,* flipping them over and under his fingers like a magician handling silver coins. With the Turk apparently distracted by his own magic, Cord moved quickly forward to attack. He feinted as if to deliver a forefist punch, then whirled into a roundhouse kick.

The target was gone as quickly as his foot left the ground. He turned, quickly set himself and found Jungar dancing left, then right, then leaping at him. Cord ducked and came up with a reverse punch as the monkey-man flew past.

Again the target was gone, and again the panther-man was flying through the air, claws flashing at Cord's face. Cord went down. On his hands and knees for an instant, he scrambled to the side and whirled to face whatever enemy was coming next.

The drum was pounding urgently now and the music was a strident wail of noise. In front of Cord all three of the opponents were stalking him; the panther-man moving to the left, the monkey-man to the right, and Changsha coming straight ahead in a low crouch. Cord feinted toward the monkey-man and leaped at Changsha with a flying kick.

His foot lashed out and hit nothing. When Cord landed, only the panther was snarling at him. Then the form suddenly became a monkey as it moved forward. Cord struck out with a side kick and whirled past. When he pivoted back, Changsha was facing him.

The Turk moved to the left and once again became a panther. Then he moved two paces to the right and became the monkey-man. For a moment all three were visible; all swaying in the same rhythm, their movements identical.

Cord didn't move. He kept his eyes only on Changsha, refusing to recognize the existence of the others. The big Turk glared back, the smile now humorless. Cord was conscious of the panther-man stalking around farther to the side, and Jungar doing the same on the other side. Cord still didn't take his eyes from Changsha.

The Turk glanced to the left and right as if watching his accomplices. Cord still didn't move. Then both the panther-man and Jungar came back into sight. Once again their movements matched Changsha's. They lifted their hands, fingers dancing, and their heads swayed from side to side to the rhythm of the music. Then, as if Cord's vision were suddenly returning to normal, they edged closer and closer to Changsha, and finally merged into the single body.

The Turk was no longer smiling as he stepped back a pace and began to circle Cord. As if he had lost his most lethal weapons, he now moved more cautiously. Cord moved with him, keeping within striking distance.

The music was no longer frantic. The drum had settled into the methodical beat again, and over the other sounds Cord now hear the richly textured tone of a flute. A hush had fallen over the beach, and even the drumbeats were now softer. Cord took a deep breath, feeling an unusual calmness spread through his body.

The Turk's eyes were narrowed and his jaw tight as he suddenly reversed the direction of his circling. At the same instant Changsha made the turn, Cord whirled forward with a roundhouse kick. There was a jarring impact, and the instep of his foot met teeth and saliva, and his heel whipped the Turk's head to the side.

With Changsha's reeling back, Cord moved in with a sharp knife-hand strike to the collarbone. He followed with a roundhouse punch to the temple.

Changsha staggered away, his arms covering his face. But he still didn't go down. Cord stuck with him and delivered another sharp blow to the spleen. Changsha finally doubled forward with a moan and stumbled away.

Cord watched for a minute as the big man staggered around the edge of the carpet. Then he leaped high in the air and jammed his foot into the back of the Turk's exposed neck. As if his nervous system suddenly stopped functioning, Changsha dropped straight to the carpet, his head twisted at a grotesque angle.

The drum was no longer beating, and the crowd was deathly silent. Cord moved across and stood over the sprawled body, waiting. From the feel of the kick, Cord knew he had not broken the man's neck. But Changsha was gasping deeply for breath, and for a full minute he didn't move. Cord was also breathing heavily, but the victory was no less delicious.

The Turk finally shifted. He slowly drew his arms in and raised himself to his hands and knees. With his head hanging, he was motionless for another minute. Then he came heavily to his feet. He wiped a hand across his mouth and gazed at the blood. Then he smiled crookedly at Cord. "Not the same Cord," he grunted.

Cord smiled. "Nòt the same Cord."

Changsha took a deep, shaky breath and lifted an arm. "The way is across the water."

Cord frowned and looked in the direction the Turk was pointing. The crowd had parted, and close to the shore a small boat was being drawn forward by what looked like monks.

It was an odd-looking boat, no more than twenty feet long. The prow curved high in the air and had a carved figure like those of the old Viking ships. At the back an intricately carved fan-like configuration rose almost as high as the prow. The twelve monks manning the vessel were all robed and hooded, six of them working the oars. The other six had stepped into the shallow water and were dragging the boat forward.

Changsha put an arm around Cord's shoulders and led him through the crowd. "The way is across the water," he repeated.

A few yards from the boat Cord stopped and looked out at the sea. He could see nothing on the horizon, nor were there any islands visible along the coast. Behind him the crowd waited silently, and Changsha gave him a questioning look. Then Cord heard the thin note from a flute drifting lightly across the water. He smiled to himself and moved forward.

The monks on shore stepped to the side, making a path for him, their heads bowed as if in prayer. None of them lifted his eyes as Cord moved past and stepped into the boat.

"Good luck," Changsha said quietly.

Cord nodded and moved to the narrow seat at the back. The six monks marched forward and dragged the boat into the water again. When it was moving, they climbed in and took their places, two in front and four behind the oarsmen.

On the beach, Changsha looked thoughtful as the boat slowly moved into deeper water. Then a faint smile crossed his bloody face, and he turned away. As he walked up the beach, the drummers and musicians began playing again. Then jugglers were suddenly tossing tenpins and plates in the air and slave girls and concubines were yelping and running back to the tents. The festivities were resuming, and Changsha's trudging steps began to pick up speed as he followed the others.

The oarsmen finally turned the boat, and they headed out to sea.

"You are Cord?" one of the monks asked over his shoulder. He was a young man with clear blue eyes that seemed to penetrate Cord's soul.

"Yes," Cord answered.

The man nodded and faced the front again.

"How did you know?" Cord asked.

The man's head lowered as if he were praying again. Cord waited, but no answer came.

"Are you taking me to Zetan?"

There was still no answer. Cord gave up and looked past the prow of the boat to the horizon. They were heading directly out to sea, but there was still no land in sight.

The six oarsmen facing him all had their eyes closed. They leaned forward and pulled back in a steady cadence, their strokes as smooth and precise as if they were locked into a single harness. Cord watched them for a while and finally leaned his head back against the fan.

Last night Changsha had said that Zetan was very, very close. Cord wondered how far very, very close was. He also wondered what position the twelve men in front of him held in Zetan's kingdom. Were they slaves—mercenary guards who protected the kingdom from intruders? All of them looked lean and hard and capable of defending themselves.

XIII

It was past noon when Cord finally spotted a small speck on the horizon. As they drew nearer, the speck broadened into a coral island several miles wide. It was entirely mountainous, and within the lush foliage of its slopes a few white buildings with gold roofs and spires stood in sharp contrast to the deep green.

Their eyes still closed, the oarsmen kept up their steady cadence, guiding the boat directly to the center of the island. Cord could now see a temple, and off to the side a meditation hall with a jewelled roof. Several buildings with marble facades and pillared colonades were visible. The whole island had a remarkably fertile appearance, and the pure white structures scattered around the slopes glistened brightly in the sun.

The monks said nothing after they pulled the boat onto the beach. Once again the six men bowed their heads and formed a double column as Cord stepped out of the boat. As he strode between them they all quickly turned and moved up the beach as if escorting a prisoner to the gallows.

Cord wondered if they would pounce on him if he turned and broke away. They moved up a gravel path that appeared to have been raked only moments before. On either side the banks were thick with flowers, and the huge pepper and eucalyptus trees almost completely blocked out the sun.

A moment later they came to a clearing, also neatly raked and landscaped. In its center a huge fountain sprayed its water into a pond of goldfish. The six men guided Cord around the pond and continued along a level walk that passed several columned buildings with massive steps. More monks were visible now, some quietly talking on the steps, others cultivating the gardens or meditating in miniature temples set back among the trees. They appeared to be all ages, from their early twenties to wrinkled old men with rheumy eyes. Their robes were in a variety of colors, from somber black and gray to rich reds, yellows, and blues.

One of the escorts touched Cord's elbow, and the double column suddenly turned up a narrower path that led into a grassy, park-like area. In the center was a low building with heavy wooden beams and what looked like sliding walls of white paper. When they reached the door, the column stopped, and the man in front gestured for Cord to enter.

It was a bathhouse. The six men marched away, and Cord moved down a corridor to a large open area that contained several baths. From the rising steam, they appeared to be of varying temperatures. Along the sides were several dressing rooms, and Cord entered one of the open doors.

Soap, stacks of fresh towels, and bottles of various shapes were resting on a broad shelf. On a small table were a bouquet of roses and a large bowl of fresh fruit. Cord smiled and sat down. Zetan might be the most deadly fighter in the world, but he was also a gracious host.

After he had washed and rinsed himself, Cord lay back in a warm pool wondering if all these comforts were another trial—another seduction designed to tempt him. Or did Zetan want to make certain his hands were not soiled when he dispensed with a challenger?

He stepped out of the pool and moved to the far end of the huge room. The water in the last bath was like that of an arctic pond. After he tested it, he jumped from the edge and plunged into the center.

The shock of being enveloped in the icy liquid sent a tremor up and down his spine. When he finally lifted his head above the surface he gasped for a minute, and then breathed deeply, forcing oxygen back into his almost numbed limbs. Then he moved to the side and climbed out.

When he finished drying himself, the six monks once again appeared. Their faces were expressionless as they waited outside the dressing room. Cord gave them a questioning look, and a man stepped forward and unfolded a brilliant red robe with gold trimmings on the edges. He held it open, and Cord slid into it. The six men did an about-face, and he followed them out the door and back to the path.

They continued their trek past the buildings and finally angled up the mountainside and into a large courtyard. A few paces inside, the men stopped, and Cord stood silently in their midst.

There were several fountains in the courtyard, all of them spouting plumes of water into circular ponds. Between them were neatly tended gardens, birdbaths, and gravel walks. There were vines and flowers everywhere, on the walls, in huge pots, some of them tangled in the foliage of the trees. In the courtyard across from Cord about thirty monks were standing quietly—all of them apparently waiting for the great man to appear.

Cord closed his eyes for a minute. From the looks of things, the final battle would be taking place shortly, and he wanted to force all thoughts and emotions out of his mind. From now on, he must depend on his past training and innate abilities. The details and procedures of the training must be forgotten, and he must count on only what his nerves and reflexes had learned from it. If Zetan turned out to be a giant or a monster of some kind, he must attack with a ferociousness he had never felt before. If Zetan was an artist like Ah Sahm, he must employ the arts of guile and deception.

Cord finally opened his eyes and gazed straight ahead. If there were drums or music, he would not hear them. If Zetan appeared in the form of a tiger, or a buffalo or a dragon, he would not be intimidated. He would fight only the man behind the disguise.

A movement higher on the mountain caught his attention, and Cord lifted his gaze. A group of monks was moving slowly down a flight of stone steps, their heads bowed as if in prayer. There were about ten of them, all except one wearing blue robes. The other man was hidden within their midst, but Cord glimpsed a flash of gold as they disappeared from sight.

None of the monks in the courtyards glanced up. Some were standing with their hands behind their backs, gazing off at the fountains. Others had their eyes closed, apparently meditating. As Cord glanced around, two monks in rust-colored robes pushed open a heavy door at the far side of the courtyard, then moved to the sides and bowed their heads. A moment later the group of blue-robed monks turned from a distant stairway and moved slowly toward the opened doors.

Cord could still not see what kind of man or beast was wearing the gold-colored garments. Most of those surrounding him were big men— at least a foot taller than he was—completely blocking Cord's view.

Once they were through the door, the group continued the unhurried pace across the courtyard. The men in front gazed evenly at Cord, but he could tell nothing from their expressions. They might have been studying him, or looking a mile past.

Cord took a deep breath and held his head high. He was ready. Whether the next few minutes meant death or victory, he had already achieved enough wisdom to make it worthwhile. As Changsha had observed, he was not the same Cord.

The group stopped a few paces in front of him.

At his left and right, the six monks quietly turned and moved away. Then one of the blue-robed men came around from the back of the group. A young man with a closely shaven head, he gazed silently at Cord for a minute, then bowed.

Cord returned the salute.

"You have sought Zetan," the young man said. "Zetan is here." He stepped aside, and the wedge of blue-robed monks separated, at last revealing the great Zetan.

Cord stared, not quite believing it. He had been prepared for anything: from a jackal-headed monster to a thick-necked three-hundred-pound brute with sledge-hammer fists. What he saw was a slender, delicate-looking man in his late sixties. As the man came forward and spread his hands in a welcoming gesture he reminded Cord of Ah Sahm. He moved with the same effortless step, and the outspread hands were smooth and slender and seemed almost like those of an artist.

"My dear Cord," the old man said, "I'm so pleased to see you." His voice was soft, but also resonant enough to carry across the courtyard.

Cord was not sure how to respond. The man was certainly more friendly than Ah Sahm had ever been. But it was hard to tell what was behind the smile and the faintly bemused eyes. A man who was a master of the martial arts could afford to toy with his opponents. And on an island like this he probably had very little in the way of amusements.

The old man stepped to the side and his hand glided across in a movement that prompted Cord to turn quickly into a fighting stance. He half expected a weapon of some kind to appear in the man's hand. Instead, from one of the big pots, Zetan deftly plucked a flower and lifted it to his face. He smiled at Cord's tense reaction.

"Extraordinary what the soil here does for the perfume," he said. Moving more slowly this time, he held the flower out to Cord.

Cord studied the man closely, noting the position of his feet and the relaxed fingers of the free hand. Then he stepped forward and took the flower.

"Do you agree?" Zetan asked.

Cord frowned, forgetting for a minute what the man had said. Then he gave the flower a quick sniff. "Yes," he answered.

Zetan looked off at the sea. "At this hour the wind arrives from the east. It's the best time of day to enjoy the scent of the roses." He smiled at Cord, then pointed at a building just above the courtyard. "That is the Temple of the Pillar of the Universe."

Cord gave the place a quick glance. It was an ornate structure that looked a thousand years old. Eight or ten monks were quietly passing in and out.

"Nice, isn't it?" Zetan asked.

"Beautiful," Cord said. "Who are the people?"

"Those monks are the near ones."

Cord relaxed a little. The smile was gone from the old man's face, and he looked thoughtful.

"They are studying the perfecting of perfection," Zetan said.

"Are you their teacher?"

The man shook his head. "Not really. We've

found that the best way is for the teacher . . . so-called . . . and the taught to produce the teaching together. What do you think?"

Cord blinked at the man, a little surprised by the question. He had come all this way to fight Zetan for possession of the Book of Wisdom. Instead of fighting, the man was asking his opinion about teaching methods. "Yes," Cord finally said. "It sounds reasonable."

The old man nodded, and once again Cord tensed as a hand came toward him. But Zetan did nothing more than clap him on the shoulder. "Do you mind strolling?" he asked.

Cord glanced at the other monks. They seemed to have lost interest in what Zetan was doing. Some were walking out the far door, chatting easily with each other. Others seemed to be discussing the flowers, or meditating.

"All right," Cord said.

The old man smiled and they walked slowly through the same archway where Cord had entered with the six monks.

They walked for almost an hour. Zetan showed him the gardens and temples and residence buildings, all the while speaking softly and respectfully. It was as if Cord were some visiting dignitary the old man was anxious to please. At times, however, the man's eyes seemed to smile and regard him with more amusement than respect.

The battle, Cord decided, would no doubt be a very formal affair. He envisioned all the monks on the island gathering in some amphitheater, and there would be no whistling or cheering. The rules would be announced, and then judges would

208

quietly give points for subtle movements and mock blows. It would probably be like the contests in which he beat Morthond—except even more rigid. It was not the kind of fighting Cord liked, but this time he would win without breaking any rules.

A disturbing question popped into his head as he reflected on the probable course of events. If the contests were to be nothing more than quiet exercises to evaluate the contestants' technical skills, why had none of the previous "seekers" ever returned? Had they all been killed in their earlier trials? Or was Zetan playing a complex and subtle game to disarm him?

"The skillful fighter," Lo Tzu had often said, "will employ whatever means he can devise to lull his opponent into a vulnerable position—from feigned injuries to a casual attitude designed to suggest he has no serious intent in the contest.

Cord wondered.

As they toured the grounds he watched the old man, noting the gestures and the movements of the feet. For his age, Zetan was remarkably agile. His movements were as quick and effortless as Ah Sahm's, and he had the added advantage of sight.

The tour ended in a small teahouse above the meditation hall. Zetan eased down on a silk pillow and Cord took a position across from him. As quickly as they were seated, four monks appeared with teacups and pots and a charcoal brazier. An intricate ceremony followed. The water was placed on the brazier and the fire was started. Then Zetan and the monks silently meditated until the water boiled. The monks then added tea leaves and herbs, each of them bowing and reciting a prayer as he performed his task. At intervals each of the four men tasted the tea, and finally cups were filled for Zetan and Cord. After another minute of meditation, the monks moved off.

Zetan smiled and lifted his cup. Cord did the same. The tea was scalding hot, but the aroma was rich and sweet. Cord sipped and returned the old man's smile as they both put the cups back on the trays.

Zetan seemed to laugh as he folded his hands in his lap. "Now, look here," he said, "you're not worried about anything, are you?"

Cord considered the question. He was not worried, but he was getting impatient. "No," he answered.

"Go on, my boy," the old man urged. "Ask. I'm sure you're a bit puzzled."

Cord took another sip of tea, then pushed the cup away. "I'm not puzzled. I want to know . . . when we fight."

The old man's eyebrows lifted. "When who fights?"

"You and I."

"About what?"

"The Book!" Cord exclaimed.

"Ahhh." Zetan sighed heavily and nodded. "The Book. The everlasting Book. What have you been told, Cord?"

Cord stared at him, wondering if this was also part of the game. "Every year someone is chosen to find you. They all set out, but they never come back."

"What does that prove?"

"It proves you are the world's greatest martial artist!"

Zetan set his teacup aside and rose, the faint smile once more on his face. "And you want to defeat the world's greatest martial artist."

"Yes," Cord said and came quickly to his feet. "When? I wish to meditate and prepare myself."

Zetan nodded and moved to the steps. "Come. We'll go to the terrace and rehearse you in the ceremony."

"What ceremony?"

The man turned and moved down the steps. "The one that precedes *your* becoming the Keeper of the Book."

"Wait!" Cord cried and hurried after him. "I don't understand."

As if propelled by some mysterious force, Zetan was already gliding along the path. Once again he reminded Cord of Ah Sahm. Cord stepped out with long strides, but he didn't seem to gain any ground.

A ceremony that precedes his becoming Keeper of the Book? What was that supposed to mean? And was Zetan really surprised to hear he was expected to fight for the Book? After all the tricks and diversions Cord had encountered in the trials, he supposed he shouldn't be too surprised to find Zetan employing similar methods.

The trail was level and followed the contour of the mountain through a densely forested area. Five minutes later they were curving out to a craggy point that extended into the sea. As they drew nearer, Zetan slackened his pace and Cord finally caught up.

A broad niche, perhaps fifty feet wide, had been carved out of the rocks, and the area was partially shaded by wind-twisted trees. Several monks seemed to be quietly enjoying the view, and they gave Zetan and Cord only casual glances.

Facing the sea at the front of the area a canopied chair was set on a large rock. Zetan moved slowly across, his eyes fixed on the expanse of ocean beyond the point. He finally stopped and smiled back at Cord. "This is the seat of harmony, Cord. Attractive, isn't it?"

"There seems to be nothing but harmony on this island," Cord said flatly.

The observation seemed to disturb the old man. He looked quickly away and his voice was soft. "Yes . . . it permeates everything here." He gazed at the sea for another minute, then smiled at Cord. "Try the seat. Go on . . . try it."

Cord moved forward to the side of the chair, not sure what was supposed to happen. But he saw no harm in sitting in the chair. He eased into it and looked around.

"Close your eyes for a moment," Zetan urged. "Come, come, you're not afraid, are you?"

Cord closed his eyes. After a moment his tensions seemed to dissolve and he almost felt sleepy. Somewhere behind them birds were chirping, and the gentle rustling of the surf below was like a soporific. Cord took a deep breath and let himself relax completely.

"Can you see your future?" Zetan asked quietly. "Endless days of peace? Mornings touched with golden sunlight . . . evenings like velvet. Is there any man who could wish for more?"

212

Cord smiled to himself. He had never spent much time enjoying golden sunlight or velvet evenings. As pleasant as they might be, they never seemed to be anything more than backdrops for more important things. He took another deep breath, then came instantly alert as something touched his chest.

The old man's finger was outthrust, and Cord had the wrist in a vise-like grip as quickly as his eyes came open. He looked up sharply at the man.

Zetan was smiling at him, his eyes once more showing amusement. He stood silently until Cord released the arm. Then he turned to one of the monks. "The Book," he said.

Cord came quickly to his feet. On the far side of the clearing one of the monks bent forward over a table and cradled something in his arms as he came toward them. Cord stared, not believing it. The object was a large book, the leather binding decorated with etched metal. The man handed it to Zetan and moved off.

"Are you good at surprises?" Zetan asked with a smile.

Cord gazed suspiciously at the book and back at Zetan. There was a big difference between a surprise and a hoax, and he couldn't believe Zetan would permit him to look at the authentic Book without a fight or some additional trial to prove himself. "I've heard about all I . . ."

Zetan moved off to a marble lectern no higher than a bench, and gently put the book down. "Beautifully embossed, isn't it?" he said.

Was it possible? Cord stared at the Book again,

213

his curiosity growing stronger than his doubts. "What . . . what's in it?"

"You've survived several trials, I'm sure," Zetan said. "And very frightening they must have been. But what you're about to see may be even more alarming . . ."

Cord was only half listening. He moved across to the lectern and gazed down at the delicately embossed cover. There were strangely primitive designs on the leather and the metal chasing. The book had to be at least two thousand years old. How many people through all those centuries had read it? Cord eased down to his knees, but didn't dare touch the Book yet. He took a deep breath, steadying himself. He thought about Lo Tzu and the other monks at the monastery, and how reverently they had always spoken of the Book. He wished they could be here with him.

The old man moved quietly to his side. "You can take my place here without looking into it," he said. "Just as I did many years ago."

Cord glanced up, but didn't respond.

"There's no need to fight me," Zetan said. "I offer you my position and possession of the Book as a reward for your accomplishments."

Cord looked at the questioning face, then shook his head. "I must look first."

A heavy sigh came from the old man, as if this was another in a long line of disappointments. Cord hardly noticed it. He reached up and ran his fingers along the embossing. Then he lightly grasped the cover and opened the Book.

He blinked uncertainly for a minute. There was

no title page, or any authors' names. There was not even paper. He was staring at a mirror—the polished reflection of his own likeness. Cord frowned and looked at Zetan.

The old man was gazing evenly at him, neither smiling nor frowning. In a shrugging gesture he lifted his hands and turned the palms up.

Cord looked back at the Book and turned the mirrored page. A second, identical mirror showed him his own confused, frowning reflection. He turned another, and another and another, seeing the same stunned face blinking back at him. The entire Book was nothing but mirrors! His heart thudding heavily, he carefully grasped the remaining mirrors and skipped to the last page. It was exactly like the others. For a full minute he stared at the final mirror. Then he closed the Book and rose.

"There is no Book," Zetan said gently. "No enlightenment outside yourself. They make their way here every year . . . the Seekers eager to slaughter me and take the Book. And when I let them see . . . like you . . . they fling it open in a blaze of expectation. And what do they find?"

"Themselves," Cord said quietly.

Zetan nodded. "Themselves."

Cord looked at the other monks, and those back at the temples and gardens. "There is nothing to take back," he said, "so they never return."

The old man nodded. "There they are . . . most of them."

They were cultivating the gardens, meditating, moving in and out of the temples.

"Others go back to the world," the old man said, "and in all manner of disguises provide the trials . . . such as you have experienced. Some of them become teachers."

A single note from a flute sounded so softly Cord wasn't certain he had heard it at first. Then a richer tone seemed to drift across from the sea. Cord nodded. "And one of them plays a silent flute that only I can hear."

Zetan smiled. "I was your age when *I* was sent to find the Book. And I became the Keeper of it. But now, you . . . Cord . . . you will be the Keeper."

The notes of the flute were louder now, and Cord smiled, looking off at the empty sea. At one time, Ah Sahm had stood on this same spot and looked into the same Book. And all the time he had been taunting Cord and challenging him in the trials, he knew exactly what Cord was going to find in the Book. Cord smiled. Then he laughed as he backed away from Zetan.

For years he had heard about the Book, and for as many years he had trained and conditioned himself to battle his way to this island that he might take possession of it and have the benefits of its wisdom. And now he had seen it. And its lesson was so profoundly simple, he couldn't stop himself from laughing.

As Cord backed away the old man gestured toward the gardens and temples and the idyllic landscape. "You'll enjoy it!" he said in a pleading voice. "The endless beauty and pleasure!"

Cord laughed harder, at the same time shaking his head to the old man's request. The sound of

216

the flute now filled his ears, and he turned and ran.

"Cord!" Zetan's anguished voice called after him. "Release me, Cord!"

XIV

Three days passed before Cord found him. On the island he was given a dugout canoe, and he reached the mainland a few hours after sunset. Without sleeping, he traveled down the coast, using the same trail on which he had met the panther-man. Then he retraced the long journey he had made with Ah Sahm.

The woman was still in her hut with the repaired wall, but there were no marauders around. From there Cord swam across the river where he and Ah Sahm had taken the ferry. On the far bank the man was building himself a new boat, and the dimwitted son was wearily dragging logs down from the mountains.

In the desert, he found no trace of the dead tree, or the man in the barrel of oil. Either he had achieved his goal and returned to his family, or the wind had swept him away.

At times Cord heard the flute. In the evenings, when he prepared his meals and meditated, the mellow notes seemed to lower the sun gently into the horizon. In the mornings, they were more lively, as if rejoicing over the dawn of another day.

On the third morning he climbed the high mountains behind the monastery where he had battled Morthond. When he reached the pass, the air was thin and a light wind seemed to bring the flute notes from somewhere nearby. Cord smiled and slowly made his way down the mountainside.

He finally saw him, a few hundred yards below. Cord continued down until he was within a stone's throw of the man. Then he stood and listened, a quiet smile on his face.

Ah Sahm was wearing the same tan robe, sitting cross-legged, the big flute held lightly in his hands. The music he was playing was soft and peaceful, a celebration of life and wisdom and contentment.

The music finally stopped. Ah Sahm sat quietly for a minute, as if gazing into the valley. Then he rose and turned his sightless eyes to Cord. A broad smile spread slowly across his face, and his voice was warm. "You looked in the Book, Cord."

"Yes," Cord answered. He moved down to the broad ledge where Ah Sahm was standing.

"What did you see?" the old man asked.

Cord smiled. "Everything."

It was a joke, and it was also as profound as the universe. They smiled at each other, both understanding and both knowing they had only begun to understand. Ah Sahm handed the flute to

Cord and sat down to listen, his eyes lightly closed.

The notes came out badly at first: a breathy sequence of dissonant sounds. Then a richly textured note was followed by another, and without thinking or consciously directing his fingers, Cord found himself playing beautiful music.

His eyes still closed, Ah Sahm came slowly to his feet. He moved in one direction and then the other, then lifted his arms and danced with a graceful, joyous rhythm.

Cord joined him. With the flute still at his lips, he swayed and turned and followed Ah Sahm through loops and circles and ballet-like pirouettes.

The sound of the flute drifted over the mountains, and the wind carried it through the valleys and across the deserts. For any who chose to hear it, it was beautiful music.

THE BEST OF THE BESTSELLERS
FROM WARNER BOOKS

HARDCORE *by Leonard Schrader (89-657, $1.95)*
The wrenching story of a deeply religious Midwest businessman who infiltrates California's porno underground in search of his missing teen-age daughter. Before his odyssey ends he has traveled to the very pit of Hell itself, fearing only that he'll find her too late.

VOICES *by John Herzfeld (89-779, $19.95)*
The "Love Story" of 1979, VOICES is the drama of a street tough from Hoboken who aspires to be a singer and who meets and comes to cherish a shy, deaf girl who yearns to become a dancer. Tender, touching and triumphant, the simplicity and honesty of VOICES speak directly to the heart.

THE BRINK'S JOB *by Noel Behn (91-108, $2.50)*
The most extraordinary robbery in American history took six years to plan and six years and $29 million to solve. This is the inside story of the infamous Brink's robbery of 1950, and it's the most fun you can have from a bank robbery without taking the money!

EVERY WHICH WAY BUT LOOSE *by Jeremy Joe Kronsberg (90-069, $1.95)*
The hilarious love story of a crazy romance between a pretty country-western singer who thrives on one-night stands and a hard fightin', hard lovin' mechanic with a truck, a pet ape, a penchant for petty theft, and a heart as big as all outdoors.

SLOW DANCING IN THE BIG CITY *by Barra Grant (89-630, $1.95)*
He was a newspaper writer who covered the hidden dramas of the city. She was a dancer, driven to perform though her every movement was wrapped in pain. Somehow, they reached each other where their memories lived. Unlikely lovers in an unforgettable love story.

THE BEST OF THE BESTSELLERS FROM WARNER BOOKS

MADE IN HOLLYWOOD by *James Bacon* *(82-913, $2.25)*

A friend and confidant to everybody who's anybody, 20-year veteran columnist Bacon tells the zaniest, bawdiest, funniest and most intimate stories about the real Hollywood. "It's all true, and this is one of the best, funniest, most titillating, most honest books ever written about Hollywood's greatest stars."
— *Sunday Magazine*

REELING *by Pauline Kael (83-420, $2.95)*

Rich, varied, 720 pages containing 74 brilliant pieces covering the period between 1972-75, this is the fifth collection of movie criticism by the film critic *Newsday* calls "the most accomplished practitioner of film criticism in America today, and possibly the most important film critic this country has ever produced."

THE MAKING OF SUPERMAN by *David Michael Petrou* *(82-565, $2.25)*

Out of today's awesome technology comes the most spectacular entertainment in the history of motion pictures. Now, go behind the scenes for a closeup of the biggest movie to come out of Hollywood in decades! Travel with the people who made SUPERMAN live! Featuring 16 pages of photographs.

ELVIS *by Jerry Hopkins (81-665, $2.50)*

More than 2 million copies sold! It's Elvis as he really was, from his humble beginnings to fame and fortune. It's Elvis the man and Elvis the performer, with a complete listing of his records, his films, a thorough astrological profile, and 32 pages of rare, early photographs!